*The Kimmage Garrison, 1916: making billy-can bombs at Larkfield*

# Maynooth Studies in Local History

SERIES EDITOR Raymond Gillespie

This volume is one of six short books published in the Maynooth Studies in Local History series in 2010. Like over 85 of their predecessors they range widely over the local experience in the Irish past. That local experience is presented in the complex social world of which it is part, from the world of the dispossessed Irish in 17th-century Donegal to political events in 1830s Carlow; from the luxury of the early 19th-century Dublin middle class to the poverty of the Famine in Tipperary; and from the political activists in Kimmage in 1916 to those who suffered in a different sort of war as their homes were bombed in South Circular Road in 1941. These local experiences cannot be a simple chronicling of events relating to an area within administrative or geographically determined boundaries since understanding the local world presents much more complex challenges for the historian. It is a reconstruction of the socially diverse worlds of poor and rich as well as those who took very different positions on the political issues that preoccupied the local societies of Ireland. Reconstructing such diverse local worlds relies on understanding of what the people of the different communities that made up the localities of Ireland had in common and what drove them apart. Understanding the assumptions, often unspoken, around which these local societies operated is the key to recreating the world of the Irish past and reconstructing the way in which those who inhabited those worlds lived their daily lives. As such, studies such as those presented in these short books, together with their predecessors, are at the forefront of Irish historical research and represent some of the most innovative and exciting work being undertaken in Irish history today. They also provide models which others can follow up and adapt in their own studies of the Irish past. In such ways will we understand better the regional diversity of Ireland and the social and cultural basis for that diversity. If they also convey something of the vibrancy and excitement of the world of Irish local history today they will have achieved at least some of their purpose.

*Maynooth Studies in Local History: Number 88*

# The Kimmage Garrison, 1916
## *Making billy-can bombs at Larkfield*

Ann Matthews

FOUR COURTS PRESS

Set in 10pt on 12pt Bembo by
Carrigboy Typesetting Services for
FOUR COURTS PRESS LTD
7 Malpas Street, Dublin 8, Ireland
www.fourcourtspress.ie
and in North America for
FOUR COURTS PRESS
c/o ISBS, 920 N.E. 58th Avenue, Suite 300, Portland, OR 97213.

© Ann Matthews and Four Courts Press 2010

ISBN 978–1–84682–259–9

Printed in Scotland
by Thomson Litho, Glasgow.

# Contents

# Acknowledgments

I came across the story of the men of the Kimmage Garrison during the course of my research for a PhD dissertation. The men of this garrison were part of the Irish diaspora; their story and the role they played in 1916 is still largely unknown.

The idea to have it published came from Billy Fitzpatrick of Pearse College, Crumlin, who encouraged me to write the story after I gave a lecture on the Kimmage Garrison at Pearse College in 2008. He suggested I should call it 'making billy-can bombs at Larkfield' so I have incorporated this into the title.

Very recently, I met Cáit Mhic Ionnraic, the daughter of John (Blimey) O'Connor, a self-described second-generation Irish cockney. He was a member of the London Volunteers and was part of the garrison. Cáit very kindly gave me a copy of her father's personal memoir and she gave me permission to use it. She also loaned me her precious photographs for this work, and I am deeply appreciative to her for this trust.

Commandant Victor Laing and his staff at the Military Archive have been supportive of this research and have always been courteous and helpful in helping me to work through the Witness Statements and the superlative Contemporaneous Documents of the Bureau of Military History.

I would very specially like to thank Professor Ray Gillespie for accepting this work for publication in this series and for his patience with my efforts.

In reading through the memories of the men of the Kimmage Garrison, I could hear echoes of the stories my mother told us as children about her memories Easter Week. She was Jenny Matthews, and in 1916, she lived in Marlborough Street. Finally, a thank you goes to my family Ali, Tommy, and Benjamin Emmett who have been living with this story for some time now.

# Introduction

The Rebellion in Dublin in 1916 has an extensive and impressive historiography, which would indicate that there is no aspect of this event unexamined. However, a group of men who played a significant part in the story of 1916 have almost disappeared from memory. These men were the members of the Irish Volunteers from Glasgow, Liverpool, and London who travelled to Dublin from late 1915 to early 1916. There appears to have been several hundred of them and when they arrived in Dublin about 90 of them settled at the Larkfield Mill in Kimmage. This mill was located in the townland of Larkfield and was the headquarters of the 4th Battalion Irish Volunteers. However, the new arrivals retained a separate identity, because there appeared to be a problem assimilating them into the existing structure of the Dublin-based battalions. The name Kimmage Garrison was a retrospective development, which came into common usage during 1940s and 1950s when 17 of the men gave their witness statements to the Bureau of Military History.

This work will draw largely on the witness statements of the Bureau to explore the social and family backgrounds of the men and to reveal how their involvement in the Irish Ireland movement in England and Scotland led to involvement with the Irish Volunteers. One of the men who gave a witness statement was Joe Good, whose statement was expanded and published by his son in 1996 under the title *Enchanted by dreams: the journal of a revolutionary*.

The personal stories of some of the men are an insight into their early involvement in the politics of Irish Ireland. They also give an insight into the aloofness with which they were treated by the membership of the Irish Volunteers and Cumann na mBan in Dublin, and this enables an understanding of their invisibility within the historiography of 1916.

The men of the Kimmage Garrison with the Irish Citizen Army formed the vanguard of the rebel army that made up the GPO headquarters garrison. The accounts by the men of their experiences during the six-day rebellion are unique and make it possible to glean insight into events leading up to Easter 1916, what was happening inside the GPO, the retreat and surrender.

This book will use also the memoir of Geraldine Plunkett Dillon, which was published by her granddaughter Honor O Brolchain in 2006 under the title *All in the blood: a memoir of the Plunkett family, the 1916 Rising and the war of Independence*. This memoir in conjunction with her witness statement to the Bureau of Military History is an excellent eyewitness account of the story of the Kimmage Garrison, and an insight into the activities of the Plunkett

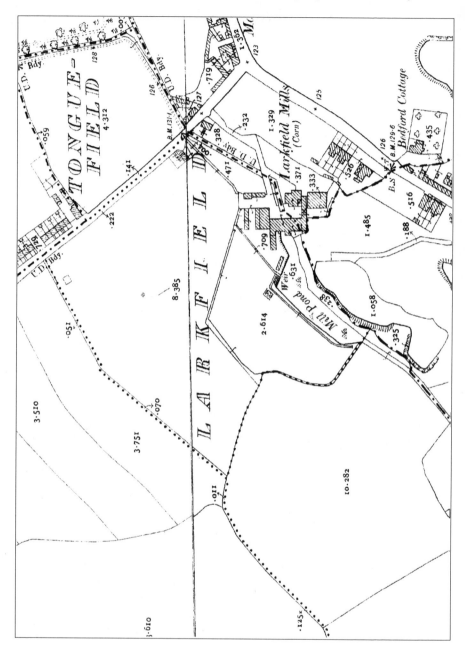

1 Map of Larkfield, courtesy of Ordnance Survey Ireland.

siblings, namely Geraldine, Joseph, George, and Jack. The files of the Royal Irish Constabulary were exceptionally useful in researching this story, in particular the aftermath of the Rebellion.

Countess Plunkett purchased the townland of Larkfield in 1913 and the story of how it became central in political and military activities between late 1915 and Easter 1916 is another important factor in the story of the Kimmage Garrison.

The book concludes by examining and exploring the changes in the townland of Larkfield when the Rathmines Township ended in 1930, and subsequently subsumed by the urbanization of Dublin City. When the Dublin City Council dedicated a public park in the area to Eamon Ceannt, the commander of the 4th Battalion Irish Volunteers, the Kimmage Garrison was effectively erased from the narrative of 1916.

2 Group photo, *c.* mid-1950s, taken at a reunion at Larkfield. Group consists of some of the men of the Garrison with their children. Courtesy of Cáit Mhic Ionnraic, daughter of John (Blimey) O'Connor

# 1. Larkfield House and Mill, 1837–1913

The Larkfield Mill was built on the boundary of the Larkfield and Kimmage townlands. The townland of Larkfield was located in the barony of Uppercross, and lay between the rural villages of Crumlin, Kimmage, and Terenure, within the Civil Parish of Crumlin. The river Poddle marked the urban boundary between the Kimmage and Larkfield townlands. In 1837, Lewis's topographical dictionary described the area as one dotted with limestone quarries and large flour mills.

The source of the river Poddle is in the hills at Cookstown in Tallaght, and fed from the Dodder River at a purpose built weir near Firhouse. In the late 19th century this stretch of river was dotted with several mills; for example, about one mile distant from the Larkfield Mill there was the Ravensdale Mill. The Poddle passed through the Larkfield townland to Tonguefield and from here channelled into the city, entering the River Liffey at Wellington Quay.

### Table 1. Ownership of Larkfield Mill, 1837–85

| Year | Name | Activity |
|------|------|----------|
| 1837–1860 | Edward Ennis | miller (corn miller) |
| 1860 | John Green | market gardener |
| 1870 | Edward Ennis | miller (corn miller) |
| 1881 | William Danford | Larkfield Flour Mill |
| 1885– | William Danford & Robert Herron | miller merchant / roller mills |
| 1880–1909 | Herron and Connolly Mill and Bakery Ltd. | miller merchant / roller mills |

Source: Land Valuation Office and *Thom's Directory*

In 1885, William Danford and Robert Herron extended and modernized the mill. The new mill building was fitted with 'a complete and improved roller plant, capable of grinding 1,000 barrels of wheat per week'.[1] A new weir was built and a mill wheel was constructed across the river Poddle, which meant that the Larkfield Mill now straddled the district electoral boundary. A three-story bakery was built adjoining the mill and this was fitted with new modern ovens. There was also a mill manager's house and ten acres of prime grassland. The house was described in the *Irish Times* as a desirable residence within a few minutes walk of the tram and it contained 'a hot and cold bath, a walled-in garden, stabling for three or four horses, and a man's room paddock'.[2] Robert Herron lived in the mill manager's house and it became known as Larkfield House. The only other inhabitants in the townland were the families who lived in four worker's cottages. When Sir William Danford died in 1886, his widow Anna sold his share of the business to Herron.

In 1890, Robert Herron went into a new partnership with Michael and Thomas Connolly. The Connolly brothers had been in the business for fifty years and owned bakery shops at King Street and Marlborough Street in Dublin. Robert Herron was an experienced baker and miller; he owned bakery shops at Lower George's Street, in Kingstown, and Rathmines in Dublin. Robert Herron was appointed Managing Director of the company with a salary of £500 a year and he remained living at Larkfield House. The new company was called Herron and Connolly Mill and Bakery Ltd, and in March it was launched on the Dublin stock exchange, with its published prospectus putting its value at £70,000. From the outset, the Larkfield mill and bakery struggled to become successful. While bread formed a significant part of the diet of the citizens of Dublin, it appears that baking bread was an exceptionally competitive business and within months the company was advertising a 'reduction in the price of its bread'.[3] In 1892, the company was reorganized, and the baking part of the operation relocated to South King Street in the city. The company was never a success and it was in addition subject to the vagaries of the Dublin Stock Exchange. Over a ten-year-period, from 1899, the company struggled to become profitable. The end came in 1909 when the company went into liquidation and its assets were sold on the instructions of the liquidator. Other bakery companies snapped up several of their bread shops. The main purchasers were Sir Joseph Downes of Downes Bakery Ltd and the Dublin Bread Company Ltd.

In 1904, the Rathmines Township subsumed the Larkfield townland. The Rathmines Township was initially created as a sanitary area in 1847 and by the end of the 19th century it had expanded to include the townlands of Rathgar, Sandymount, Ranelagh, Milltown, and the barony of Uppercross. In 1911, the Larkfield townland had a total population of 25 people. At this time, Larkfield Mill and House came within the postal district of the Rathmines Post Office, and its official postal address was Dark Lane, Kimmage. A land agent named Richard Huggard and his two sisters occupied Larkfield House. In the two (three-room) cottages located in Dark Lane there were two families. One was James Fagan, his wife and their four children, whose ages ranged from 8 to 16 years. The second cottage was the home of William Finley, his wife Emily and seven of their children, whose ages ranged from 11 years to 22. On the Kimmage side of the Larkfield electoral boundary, there was another three-room cottage occupied by two families, namely Thomas Finlay who with his wife Mary and their baby occupied one room, while Patrick Boyle with his wife Mary and their two young children occupied the other two rooms. Boyle was a carpenter and described himself as a representative of Herron Connolly. In 1913, Countess Josephine Plunkett took a lease on Larkfield House and Mill from Sir Fredrick Shaw at £13 19s. 6d. a year. The lease also included some land outside the Larkfield townland. Countess Plunkett was the wife of George Nobel Plunkett (a papal Count) and they had seven children. Their family home was at Fitzwilliam Street in Dublin. The countess was a wealthy woman in her own right, having inherited many properties in the prestigious area of south Dublin from which she had significant rental income. On her marriage, she retained total control of her inheritance and went on to speculate by acquiring other properties. When Countess Plunkett took the lease on the Larkfield property her sole intention was to generate rental income by sub-letting the property.

By this time, 'the faded sign of Herron Connolly and Co. was still hanging on the front of the building'.[4] The mill manager's house was occupied by John Robinson, his wife and baby daughter, who had been born at the house in June 1913. The Countess set about making some changes. According to Geraldine Plunkett Dillon, her mother dismantled the internal structure of the mill's boiler house and created two four-roomed cottages. She installed in each cottage an indoor lavatory, a sink, a bathroom with a bath and a small range to heat the water. These would have been absolute luxury for any cottage dweller at that time. James O'Neill, who was the Plunkett's gardener and coachman, rented one of the cottages. He was paid £1 a week and his rent for the cottage was 6s. The townland at this time also contained two quarries and an outdoor shooting range, which was used by a clay pigeon shooting club.

Within the mill, there were now two businesses in operation. James and George Quinn, who were poplin weavers, worked with their loom making silk poplin. Another brother, Thomas, who was a baker, was operating a small bakery. Geraldine Plunkett Dillon said that these men worked very hard, 'setting the sponge all night, and then by day, one of them drove the bread cart while the second brother wove the poplin'.[5] At this time, the shooting range was rented to William Kavanagh & Son, who was a gunsmith. Kavanagh's business was located at 12 Dame Street Dublin and was described in *Thom's Directory* as a manufacturer of gunpowder. A man called Andy Clerkin rented the pastureland for grazing his horses.

In 1914, Geraldine Plunkett Dillon moved to Larkfield, into the cottage next to James O'Neill. She had become the main carer for her brother Joseph, who was suffering from advanced glandular tuberculosis (TB); she moved with him from the family's home in Fitzwilliam Street to the Larkfield cottage so that he could have clean air. At this time, Geraldine was working as a researcher for Professor Hugh Ryan at UCD (on the synthesis of vanillin), and she travelled every day to Earlsfort Terrace by tram, while Joseph mostly remained at the cottage because he was frail and needed 24-hour nursing care. Geraldine also brought the family housekeeper with them and they employed a nurse. Because the cottage was too small to accommodate her, she lived across the mill yard in the man's paddock room. Joseph continued with his writings and 'was able to make use of the printing press that had been set up there'.[6] In the late winter of 1914 or early 1915 they left Larkfield and returned to the family home in the city.

By autumn of 1915, the Quinn brothers had gone out of business. The Robinson family vacated Larkfield House, and Geraldine moved the Plunkett family into the house. She described it at this time as a 'beautiful middle-size house containing twelve rooms, with a garden full of roses and a hen yard'.[7] Her brothers Joseph, George, Jack, and their father Count Plunkett joined her at Larkfield. Her mother was in the USA at this time. By this time Joseph was a member of the Irish Republican Brotherhood (IRB) Military Council and Director of military operations of the Irish Volunteers.

Joseph Plunkett took his responsibilities seriously, and spent much of 1915 travelling to and from Germany, having medical treatment while simultaneously meeting with Roger Casement and seeking German support for the Irish cause. When he was in Dublin, he stayed at Larkfield; because he was physically frail, it became his headquarters. Consequently, the executive of the Irish Volunteers held several meeting at Larkfield and Geraldine was privy to much intelligence, because Joseph appears to have trusted her absolutely. By early 1916, the activity at the Larkfield Mill became more intense as it was transformed into an armed camp, with about 90 men living on the premises. These men comprised the ranks of the Irish Volunteers from England and Scotland as well as a handful of men who were on the run in Ireland. They lived and worked at the Larkfield Mill, and they formed the group that in retrospect became known as the Kimmage Garrison.

## 2. The Irish Volunteers and the creation of the Kimmage Garrison

Sometime in early 1914, Larkfield became the operational base for the 4th Battalion of the Irish Volunteers. This came about through the activities of Joseph Plunkett and his brothers George and Jack. Joseph had induced his brothers to join the Irish Volunteers, with Jack joining the organisation while still a student at Clongowes Wood College, in Kildare. The first meeting of the 4th Dublin Battalion, Irish Volunteers, took place at the Larkfield Mill on 21 January 1914; the mill was established as the battalion's headquarters. The volunteers had use of the shooting range at Larkfield as well as the top storey of the three-storey bakery. This space, which became know as the 'Hall', measured 60 by 35 feet. The 4th Battalion advertised their activities in the Irish Volunteer in April 1914 saying:

> The battalion HQ is at Larkfield Kimmage Road. There are full facilities for indoor and outdoor drill and on fine moonlit nights, the men drill in the open. All the companies of this battalion drill at Larkfield.[1]

The 4th Battalion consisted of six companies and on weeknights each one held training sessions at the Hall, while at weekends they met for classes in first-aid, signalling, fieldwork, and drilling. Geraldine Plunkett Dillon recalled that on occasions when there were accidents during rifle practice, her cottage became a first-aid post. The volunteers used the grazing land for drilling exercises. They were a very mixed bunch, with some of them 'wearing morning coats, and striped trousers, some in uniform, while others were in rags'.[2] This echoes Ernie O'Malley's description of the members of the volunteers as 'university students, government clerks, businessmen, skilled labour, unskilled labour, newsboys and at very bottom there were the out-of-works, and the guttees'.[3]

In her memoir, Geraldine recalled that 'early one September morning in 1914 about 6,000 men gathered at the mill yard at Larkfield under the leadership of Thomas McDonagh, and Patrick Pearse, to take part in a route march and manoeuvres in the Dublin Mountains'.[4] Within weeks of this event, the Irish Volunteers had split and the 4th Battalion held the decisive meeting at Larkfield; in the aftermath, the membership was significantly reduced. Cumann na mBan, the Irish Volunteer women's auxiliary organization, were not at any time involved with events at Larkfield. The Inghinidhe na hÉireann branch of the organization was officially attached to the 4th Battalion, but they met at 6 Harcourt Street, the headquarters of the Sinn Féin party. Geraldine Plunkett Dillon said that she had put her name forward to join the organisation, but that Joseph advised her not to join because he wanted 'to use her as a messenger'.[5] This was to become a common practice during the War of Independence when Michael Collins instructed his female messengers not to join the organisation.

From late 1915, the Irish Volunteers from Britain began to drift to Ireland, with some of the men being billeted at the Larkfield Mill. According to Joseph Gleeson, the decision to use the Larkfield Mill as an Irish Volunteer camp came about in January 1916 at a meeting of the Supreme Council of the IRB. He said that he went to Larkfield to organize the camp and prepare it for the arrival of the volunteers, accompanied by Eoin McNeill and a volunteer he named as Fitzgibbon. Gleeson said that the old mill building was designated for use as the main camp area. The volunteers who came from Scotland and England comprised men who had emigrated from Ireland and the sons and grandsons of Irish emigrants. As the Irish Volunteers organized within the Irish communities in Britain there was a simultaneous move to organize branches of Cumann na mBan.

The men of the Kimmage Garrison who gave witness statements to the Bureau of Military History described how their participation in Irish nationalist politics was rooted in personal family history, and in the Irish Ireland cultural organizations within their respective communities. The GAA and the Gaelic League enabled a strong ambience of Irish nationalist identity to evolve within sections of the Irish community in Britain. These communities were used as recruiting grounds for the IRB. The issue of IRB membership dominates the narratives of these men and it would be reasonable to suggest that the GAA and Gaelic League were hijacked. Arthur Agnew said that 'recruiting for the IRB took place among the Irish Volunteers and the various Irish societies existing in Liverpool at that time'.[6]

Arthur Agnew, who was born in Liverpool, said there was an active IRB circle in operation in that city and their meetings were held at the Gaelic League rooms. He was involved with Irish politics through his grandfather, who was active in Irish politics and held the position of IRB Centre for the north of England. In his witness statement Agnew said that he was sworn into the IRB in 1910 as a member of the Bootle Circle of the IRB, after which he was ordered with others to join the local rifle clubs and make full use of their facilities. In 1914 he was ordered to join the Irish Volunteers branch in Liverpool and to take hold of key positions. At that time, Agnew believed that 'the Irish Volunteers was really started by the IRB'.[7]

Joseph Gleeson from Liverpool said that his family was steeped in the history of the Fenian movement; one of his earliest memories as a small child was being brought to hear a lecture by O'Donovan Rossa. Gleeson joined the

Gaelic League and was an active member of the GAA. He said that he encountered the IRB though the GAA and that he was 'sworn into the Bootle Circle of the IRB by John Fitzgerald'.[8] He joined the Liverpool branch of the Sinn Féin party and when the IRB created a new Circle, Gleeson was put in charge of recruitment. By 1913 he had risen within the ranks of the IRB to become representative for the north of England. This involved regular attendance at the meetings of the Supreme Council of the IRB and brought him to Dublin every three months. In his witness statement, he described the first meeting that he attended at Clontarf in Dublin, and named the entire membership of the Supreme Council.

**Table 2. Supreme of Council of the IRB, 1913**

| Name | Centre |
| --- | --- |
| Sean McDermott | Connacht |
| Bulmer Hobson | Leinster |
| Diarmuid Lynch | Munster |
| Dinny McCullough | Ulster |
| Joseph Gleeson | North of England |
| Mulholland | Scotland |
| P.S. O'Hegarty | South of England |

Source: BMH, Joseph Gleeson Witness statement, p. 4

Gleeson said that Mulholland resigned soon after this meeting and the Council then co-opted four new members, who he said were Dan Branniff, Seamus Deakin and Tom Clarke; he was unable to recall the fourth name.

Joe Good, who lived in London, said in his statement that he was a member of the Gaelic League. In 1913, he came across the news of the formation of the Irish Volunteers while reading *An Claideamh Soluis*, which was surreptitiously distributed in the branches of the Gaelic League in London. Good had an interesting perspective on the membership of the Gaelic League, saying that

> The Gaelic Leaguers were quite a crowd for me: they were mainly civil servants and schoolteachers, a step up the social ladder from my usual associates, but still, if you try to learn Irish they accepted you like a brother.[9]

John O'Connor was born in 1896 in the parish of St Anne's in the east end of London. His grandparents were from Kerry and Galway and had left Ireland in the aftermath of the Famine. Both of O'Connor's parents were born in east London. He said that 'the parish was like an Irish colony' and that his 'family lived in an Irish Ireland atmosphere most of the time'.[10] He described his family as musical and said that his parents taught him and his siblings Irish history, music and songs. His parents were tailors and worked from home; they sang as they worked and the children absorbed the Irish musical tradition. When John was old enough he 'joined Irish Clubs and attended the ceilidhe organized by the United Irish League, Conradh na Gaelige and the Irish Volunteers'.[11] He joined the London Company of the Irish Volunteers; he said it had a membership of about 500 but that in the aftermath of the split in 1914 it was reduced to 50. The London volunteers moved to Dublin in January 1916 in twos and threes so as not to attract any attention; John travelled on 15 January. He said that '95% of the men had no money or relatives in Ireland and so they were brought to the Larkfield mill'.[12]

Seamus Robinson, who was born in Belfast, came from a Fenian family. His maternal granduncle was a Fenian who had left Ireland for the USA in 1867, and his paternal grandfather was a Fenian who had left Ireland and settled in France, where Robinson's father was born. Around 1870 the family returned to Belfast and then in 1903 moved to Scotland. John McGallogly, who was born in Lanarkshire in Scotland, said that his connection to the national movement came about when his older brother James induced him into membership of the IRB.

The main role of the Glasgow volunteers appears to have been to acquire guns and ammunition. There were 26 members of the Glasgow volunteers plus two women actively involved in a systematic plan to acquire and move considerable quantities of arms and explosives to Dublin. The two women were Margaret Skinnider, who was captain of the Glasgow-based Ann Devlin branch of Cumann na mBan, and a member who is named only as Miss O'Neill. Margaret Skinnider's parents were James Skinnider, a mason journeyman, and his wife Jane (nee Dowd). Margaret was born on 28 May 1892 in the working class area of Coatbridge near Glasgow, an area of mining and heavy industry. The Coatbridge community contained a significant Irish population, with some of the men of the Kimmage Garrison coming from the area. Skinnider said that she carried 'detonators for bombs in her hat with the wires wrapped around her, beneath her coat'.[13] Lizzie Morrin, another member of Glasgow Cumann na mBan, was a dressmaker and made waistcoats and jackets with hidden pockets to hide the guns and ammunition.

According to Seamus Robinson, 'the Fianna organisation in Glasgow was very active and heavily involved in raiding munitions factories and mines for explosives'.[14] He said that around the end of 1915, he noticed a sense of suppressed excitement among the Fianna lads, and an increase in their activities. The raids became almost barefaced, apparently because the men remained undetected for some time. Their final raid, which Robinson described as their 'grand finale', was on a colliery at Uddington where they got 'a huge haul of explosives'.[15] John McGallogly, who worked at the Uddington colliery, became involved in this raid because his older brother James, a member of the Glasgow Volunteers, had asked him to help them gain access to the powder magazine of the colliery. John met the raiding party one Saturday night, but 'James failed to show up and so John took part in the raid'.[16] The other members of the raiding party group were Joe Robinson, Seamus Reader, Alex Carmichael, Frank Scullen, and Cormac Turner. There were two tons of explosives on the premises, but the men could only remove about two hundredweight because their escape route involved using a tram and they did not want to draw attention to themselves. This caused McGallogly to observe that they were a relatively unorganized group of raiders. Having acquired the explosives, they needed detonators; some weeks later John led a raid on another colliery but as there were less detonators than they expected they also removed a load of gelignite. This raid was at the colliery of Addie and Sons.

On 15 January 1916 the men 'removed 90 pounds of dynobel (a high-strength, low-density explosive), and 40 pounds of arkite, which was an explosive that was composed of 52% nitro-glycerine, 22.5% potassium nitrate, 3.5% nitro-cotton, 7% wood meal and 15% ammonium oxalate'.[17] During the raid, Joe Robinson accidently dropped his trade society card and five days later he was arrested at his father's home in 10 Robson Street. Here the police found a list of nine names and addresses of contacts in Dublin as well as a telegram from Seamus Reader in Dublin informing Robinson that he had arrived safe and well. On his return to Glasgow Reader was arrested and some of the stolen explosives were found at his home. Joe Robinson and Seamus Reader were interned in Edinburgh Castle but were later moved to Reading Jail. Seamus Robinson said that 'soon after this episode there was a mass movement of the Glasgow Volunteers to Dublin'.[18]

One of the gang, named as Cormac Turner, took some of the explosives to Liberty Hall in Dublin; a suggestion was made that he be sent to Larkfield. However, Milo McGarry objected to this on the basis that Larkfield was an Irish Volunteer camp and presumably, as a man connected to Liberty Hall, Turner could not be trusted. While the Irish Citizen Army and the Irish Volunteers professed to have one goal in common, the freedom of Ireland, their political philosophy was very different and consequently there was no *esprit de corps* among them. The problem of Cormac Turner was solved after some negotiations took place between Thomas McDonagh and James Connolly; according to McGarry, this incident took place 'about the time that an agreement was arrived at between the Irish Volunteers and the Citizen Army'.[19] This is a reference to the so-called kidnapping of James Connolly in late January 1916, an episode that has been discussed and speculated on by many historians without any firm conclusion being drawn. Geraldine Plunkett Dillon has added another interesting dimension to this story, which appears to suggest that perhaps Connolly was held somewhere in the Larkfield complex.

In late January 1916, James Connolly went missing for a few days when he spent time closeted with the senior members of the Irish Volunteers. Apparently Connolly's assertive and aggressive language about starting a revolution made the Irish Volunteers nervous that he would go it alone with the Irish Citizen Army. They needed to bring him on board with their plans so that both armies could work together for the same cause.

Joseph Plunkett was involved with the kidnapping of Connolly and he told Geraldine the whole story. She said that in January Joseph had stayed out all night and she was worried about him because his health was so precarious. He told her they had kidnapped James Connolly. Apparently, the Volunteers had tried to make several appointments to meet with Connolly and he always ignored them, so the Irish Volunteer Military Council kidnapped him to have a conversation. One evening as Connolly left Liberty Hall he was approached by two members of the Irish Volunteer Military Council (accompanied by two unarmed guards), who invited Connolly to accompany them. Connolly asked them if they were kidnapping him and, according to Geraldine, this is how it came to 'be called a kidnapping'.[20] She said that they brought Connolly to a house in Dolphin's Barn where he met with the rest of the council, with the exception of Tom Clarke.

They talked for some days and Connolly, who apparently had a habit of walking up and down as he talked, spent almost the entire time talking. When it was over, 'he told someone that he must have walked over forty miles that day and of course it was thought he must have been forty miles away'.[21] Connolly was now an acknowledged member of the joint Military Council of a new rebel army comprising the Irish Citizen Army and the Irish Volunteers. Cormac Turner was now allowed to stay at Larkfield.

In February 1916, Seamus Robinson and 'five or six other members of the Scottish volunteers left Glasgow for Dublin'.[22] John McGallogly and his brother James were on the run from the police in Scotland and left for Belfast, where they met up with other members of the Glasgow volunteers. From there they travelled to Dublin with two other unnamed volunteers; none of the men had been in Dublin previously. They decided to go to Tom Clarke's shop in the centre of Dublin, but were unable to find it because they did not have the actual address. They did, however, have the address of Countess de Markievicz, and went to Rathmines where McGallogly said that:

> From the moment we arrived, she was in a flutter. Ten minutes after she told us we would have to leave, as she had just got word from Volunteer sources that the house was to be raided for two men from Glasgow. She made no useful suggestion as to what we were to do when we left.[23]

Her nervousness was understandable because her house was on the list captured by the police in Glasgow. In January 1916 the police had carried out a simultaneous raid on all premises on the list and at the de Markievicz home they found 950 .22 cartridges, a hand-printing press, and a quantity of anti-British literature. The police believed the explosives stolen in Glasgow had been on the premises but had been moved when word of Joe Robinson and Seamus Reader's arrests reached Dublin. De Markievicz was not arrested.

Meanwhile, John and James McGallogly left her house and wandered back to the city centre. They decided to seek out Sean McDermott and went to the offices of the newspaper *Nationality*, but it was closed. There was a boxing club in the same building; the men enquired there for Sean McDermott, and the club had a member of that name. The two men were invited to arrange a fight, but they left and McGallogly commented 'we were not looking for the kind of fight they had to offer'.[24] By 10.00 p.m., the men were sitting outside Liberty Hall when one of them recalled seeing a Cumann na mBan poster outside the office of *Nationality* advertising a meeting at Parnell Square. Here they met Kathleen Clarke and she arranged for Sean McDermott to come and meet them. McGallogly and his brother were taken first to Dundrum and then moved around quite a bit until they were sent to work at the De Selby Quarries at Brittas near Tallaght. The job involved digging rock out of the mountainside using explosives. This was not a happy experience for McGallogly, who said that they 'spent the night in damp beds in a wooden hut and started work at 6 a.m. without having anything to eat'.[25] They had a break three hours later for breakfast, but the men did not have any food and no means of getting any, so McGallogly left and travelled back to Dublin. He then moved to the home of the Ryan family in Ballybough; the men were under orders to keep away from the city centre and not to go out at after dark. In early April, two weeks before the rebellion, they were moved to the camp at Kimmage.

Arthur Agnew said that when he got his got his conscription notice in March 1916, he left Liverpool immediately for Dublin. He was carrying a note of introduction to Volunteer Headquarters at Dawson Street, where he met Sean McDermott and The O'Rahilly. Joe Good also recalled leaving London when conscription was imminent and after learning that several members of the London volunteers had left for Dublin; he said that 'Michael Collins ordered me to move to Larkfield, Kimmage'.[26]

Seamus Robinson did not include Michael Collins in his list of the Kimmage Garrison. However, Collins surfaces constantly in the statements of the men who comprised the garrison and these make it clear that they perceived him as a member. In addition, Michael Collins had been appointed to the Military Staff of the Irish Volunteers, with specific responsibility for the Kimmage Garrison. Michael Collins left Cork for London in 1905 and became an active member of the Gaelic League and the GAA in that city. According to Tim Pat Coogan, he was sworn into the IRB by Sam Maguire in November

3 *From left:* Ernie Nunan and John 'Blimey' O'Connor. Courtesy of Cáit Mhic
Ionnraic, daughter of John 'Blimey' O'Connor, *c.*1916

1909, and enrolled in the Number 1 Company of the London Irish Volunteers
in 1914.[27] His presence in the various Irish Ireland organizations in London
is a common thread in the witness statements of the London volunteers. In
his autobiography *Enchanted by dreams*, Joe Good said that when he enrolled
in the Irish Volunteers unit in London, Collins was one of the rank-and-file,
but that within a week was promoted 'to section leader'.[28] Denis Daly from
Cahirciveen in Co. Kerry was working for the British post office in London
and joined the IRB in 1913; he said that 'the centre of his IRB circle was P.S.
Hegarty and that from 1912 to 1916 he was great friends with Michael
Collins'.[29]

Michael Collins never lived at Larkfield. He took lodgings at Mountjoy
Street in the city, but was continually in and out of Larkfield right up to Easter
Week. He was at Larkfield on a daily basis because Geraldine Plunkett Dillon
employed him to sort out her mother's chaotic financial affairs; she paid him
a salary of one pound a week, the same wage received by James O'Neill, the
Plunkett's coachman/gardener. Geraldine Plunkett Dillon's observations of
Collins at this time are very interesting. She said that apart from his knowledge
of Irish history, he read too little and had never read fiction, so Joe spent a lot
of time talking to him and introduced him to literary reading. She also
described his apparent lack of social finesse, saying he was 'unsophisticated
socially', but 'exceptionally good at finance, and his business judgment was
excellent'.[30] Collins dined with the family every day, and he told her it took
him a week or two to be able to follow the conversation around the lunch or
tea table. Geraldine made a comment about Collins, saying 'when we hear
people say he was rough afterwards we could not believe it, because he was
invariably pleasant in our home'.[31] It was apparently within this ambience that
Collins developed a firm friendship with Joseph Plunkett. However, the
volunteers who made up the rank-and-file of the Kimmage Garrison had
different experiences.

# 3. Life at the Kimmage Volunteer Camp

Geraldine Plunkett Dillon recorded her impression of the first group of volunteers to arrive at Larkfield, saying 'suddenly one morning about forty young men descended on us'.[1] Soon after their arrival, the men from Liverpool set about helping her to build dams and trenches to redirect the flood water from the Dodder and the Poddle, which had almost swamped Larkfield in October 1915. These men were the advance guard of the Kimmage Garrison, and Geraldine christened them the Liverpool Lambs. George Plunkett was appointed officer in charge of the camp, with John King as quartermaster.

According to Joe Good, when the men from Liverpool arrived at Larkfield they subscribed voluntarily to their own maintenance, and he said that 'for some time they did not receive any assistance from the Irish Volunteers or any kindred organisation, but they harboured and fed Volunteers from other parts of England who came without funds to accommodate or keep them'.[2] John McGallogly's recollection was that the initial organization of Larkfield as an armed camp was chaotic, and that it remained disorganized 'until the men sent to Kimmage put it right'.[3]

The men who lived at Kimmage were also self-sufficient in the domestic sense. Their initial non-existent cooking skills made their early efforts at cooking disastrous, but apparently they learned quickly. Geraldine Plunkett Dillon recounted how the men acquired an agricultural boiler to boil a stew; one day George came into the house to ask her how long it took to boil potatoes and she told him three-quarters of an hour, to which he replied 'they should be boiled now, it's three hours since they started'.[4] However, the men soon became proficient cooks. Their sleeping quarters, located in the barn, were basic; George Plunkett complained to Geraldine that the men were 'a handful because they grumbled all the time, especially at having to sleep in the barn', and he solved the issue by 'bringing his mattress to the barn and sleeping there with the men'.[5] John McGallogly said that when he arrived at Kimmage in early 1916 'the sleeping quarters were not up to luxury hotel standard and most of the Glasgow men had simply put their mattresses together and made one huge bed' and he considered himself 'fortunate in having an outside position'.[6]

John O'Connor said that the men at Larkfield were kept busy training like regular disciplined troops, and 'a guard was mounted on the camp day and night and the men alternated between doing guard duty and making ammunition'.[7] The men found ways of entertaining themselves; in the evenings they played cards, and chess. Some nights they held campfire concerts and it was at one of these concerts that O'Connor acquired the nickname 'Blimey'.[8] The Larkfield Mill was effectively transformed into a munitions manufacturing depot, which produced weaponry for the rebel army. Some of the men were sent to work for the De Selby Quarries in Tallaght to gain experience in the use of explosives and acquire some gelignite. The production of munitions at Larkfield was on a significant scale and sometimes the men worked (unpaid) in 24-hour shifts. They supplied this weaponry to the four Dublin battalions. The men of the Kimmage Garrison had a wide range of skills suited to this work because several of them were plumbers, carpenters, and electricians.

The *de facto* Larkfield munitions factory produced a range of weapons and some of the witness statements are very detailed in this regard. The men at Kimmage had in their possession a supply of Howth rifles and some Lee Enfield rifles. For these they made buckshot and refilled the cartridges with this shot on a large scale. This filling was made with what the men called 'large slugs', made up with nails and lumps of metal. The volunteers acquired the lead for this work from scrap-yards around the city, buying it in small amounts and carrying it on hand-carts to Larkfield through the city streets. On occasion, they received small parcels of lead from the men of the 4th Battalion. The men also made hand grenades using sections of cast iron downpipe, used tin cans, and billy cans. Joe Good described this activity and said:

> These were made of sections 2-inch by 4-inch long of cast iron downpipe with a flange end through which a long bolt was passed. A small hole penetrated one of the flanges, through which the fuse was inserted. The fuse was of sulphur or match description, that is to say, one struck it on some abrasive material before it was fit to throw. It was estimated to be a three second bomb.[9]

The munitions factory also produced lead pellets; owing to their rudimentary machinery 'the pellets were apt to have a ragged fringe of lead, these fringes we carefully trimmed off lest it should be said that we fired dumdum'.[10] At the peak of their production, on one night they produced 5,000 lead pellets and 24 hand grenades. John McGallogly said 'part of the work consisted of fitting six-foot handles to half-inch socket chisels which were to be used as lances'.[11]

Michael Collins occasionally oversaw the work at the mill, but the workers did not always welcome him. According to Joe Good, Collins displayed 'a lack of the most elementary knowledge of mechanics and made himself unpopular, because when he visited the men he was aggressive in his manner and harried the men to speed up the work'. Good said, 'I was impressed by the sense of hurry and earnestness in Michael Collins, although I had little sympathy with his drastic methods for getting the work done, since he was abusive to us' and he said that while 'the men of the Kimmage Garrison admired Collins, he was not well liked'.[12] In the midst of all this, Thomas Dillon (Geraldine's fiancé) and Rory O'Connor set up the Larkfield Chemical Company in part of the old mill building. They planned apparently to manufacture phenol (also known as carbolic acid) and ordered a vacuum distilling plant for the production of the phenol from the Scottish company Blair Campbell and Mclean.

Meanwhile, at Patrick Pearse's school St Enda's in Rathfarnham another weapons-manufacturing factory was in operation. According to Eamonn Bulfin, when the Volunteers were founded in Rathfarnham most of the older students at St Enda's joined the Rathfarnham Company, especially those who had been sworn into the IRB. In 1916, Bulfin was living at St Enda's while studying for a degree in science. He said in his witness statement that in 1915 the volunteer unit at St Enda's began making munitions under the direction of Peadar Slattery. They made shot gun ammunition and hand grenades; 'shot gun ammunition was about the size of a small pea, made from lead melted down and run into moulds made from plaster of Paris'. Willie Pearse made these moulds, belying the image presented of him within the historiography of 1916 as the passive younger brother of Patrick. The grenades made at St Enda's were, according to Bulfin, 'a fuse type' and contained 'potassium chlorate and some phosphorous, the fuse was brought up through the top of the canister, and this was bolted down, with the fuse showing out the top of the canister'.[13] They continued making the munitions up to Holy Week, when Dr Kathleen Lynn transported them to Liberty Hall in her car.

In April 1916 the number of men at Kimmage grew to 91 volunteers (see Table 3).

### Table 3. Origins of the men of the Kimmage Garrison

| Location | number |
|---|---|
| Liverpool | 37 |
| Glasgow | 19 |
| London | 17 |
| Manchester | 14 |
| Tullamore | 2 |
| Dublin | 2 |
| Total | 91 |

Source: BMH, Seamus Robinson witness statement.

The two men from Dublin were the brothers Michael and Francis Flanagan from Moore Street, where they lived and worked as poulterers. They were on the run from the police and had moved to Glasgow, but returned Dublin with the Glasgow volunteers and went to Larkfield. The Tullamore men were Peadar Bracken and Seamus Brennan, who were also on the run from the police. Bracken and Brennan arrived at the Larkfield camp after a serious ruckus between the RIC and the Irish Volunteer Company in Tullamore.

In his witness statement to the Bureau of Military History Peadar Bracken said his introduction to Irish Ireland came about when he joined the Gaelic League and Cumann na Gael in Tullamore. He claimed that the latter was a cover for IRB activity; when he was 18-years-old, William Kennedy, who was the centre for the IRB circle in Tullamore, had sworn him into the IRB. Bracken was involved in organising a branch of Sinn Féin in Tullamore in 1906 and went to Australia in 1910. He returned to Ireland in September 1914 in the immediate aftermath of the split in the Irish National Volunteers and joined the Irish Volunteers. After the split in 1914, the Tullamore branch of the Irish Volunteers managed to hold on to some arms and ammunition, which comprised two Lee Enfield rifles, 600 rounds of ammunition, 19 revolvers and about 200 rounds of ammunition.

The volunteers continued training and parading in public under the guidance of an ex-British army drill instructor. They attended training camps and in August 1915 Peadar Bracken attended lectures in Dublin 'given by James Connolly and Thomas McDonagh on street fighting and other tactics'.[14] In late 1915, they added to their war-chest with a couple of Mark III Lee Enfield rifles, acquired from British soldiers; from another source they secured gelignite with detonators and fuses. By 1916, the Volunteer company in Tullamore had rebuilt its membership and was in the process of creating a brigade area. They had continued to build their arsenal and had added another two Mauser rifles with 200 rounds of ammunition, seven Martini Henry rifles and ten shotguns with about 100 rounds. Peadar Bracken was appointed company Captain, and he said that at this time the IRB circle in Tullamore had dwindled and was virtually nonexistent.

In March 1916, an incident occurred in Tullamore that led to Brennan and Bracken leaving town and going on the run. Hostility towards the members of Sinn Féin and the Volunteers by a section of the population was smouldering and on 20 March it culminated in an attack on their meeting rooms. Two days earlier at the local railway station some local men serving with the 7th Battalion Leinster Regiment were leaving for Europe; insults had been traded between the volunteers and a number of women who were taking leave of their husbands. The following day, a similar incident took place at a hurling match. According to the *Irish Times*, a hurling match was held to raise money for the Wolfe Tone memorial fund and the local branch of Cumann na mBan had organized a flag day to raise money at the match. As the women and girls selling the flags moved through the crowd, someone attempted to snatch a flag from the lapel of an unnamed man. A confrontation developed and it ended with a revolver being drawn.

On the following evening, some members of Cumann na mBan were at the volunteer hall counting the proceeds when a hostile group gathered outside. In his witness statement Peadar Bracken said that the crowd comprised 'mostly the wives and hangers-on of the British army'.[15] Bracken and Joe Weafer escorted the women home for their own safety and then returned to the hall. At this point, the crowd had grown and some were carrying Union flags and singing songs which were apparently insulting to Sinn Féin. The two men initially perceived the situation as a juvenile prank and continued to make their way back to the hall through the crowd. However, the exchanges between some of the women in the crowd and the two men became more aggressive; as they reached door of the building some of the crowd began throwing stones breaking some of the windows. Bracken fired a shot over the heads of the crowd and the mob then attempted to rush the stairway. He fired a second time, which he said 'had the effect of quietening the crowd for a while' and the volunteers inside the hall tried to take advantage of the lull and make their escape from the building.[16] However, they were stopped by the arrival of the RIC.[17] The *Irish Times* report said that 'some of the Sinn Féiners drew revolvers while others used hurleys' and that 'the parties came to handgrips and a regular "*mêlée*" ensued'.[18] The scuffle lasted about ten minutes and the police arrested four of the volunteers, 'while others made it to the street where they were assaulted by the mob, with Seamus Brennan in particular experiencing severe treatment'.[19]

Two members of the RIC also received serious injuries. When the police arrived at the hall they were led by four senior officers: District Inspector Fitzgerald, Head Constable Stuart, County Inspector Crane, and Sergeant Aherne. The volunteers inside the building were ordered by the police to 'fall in', but they refused to comply and another scuffle ensued, this time between the volunteers and the police officers. Once again, Peadar Bracken drew his revolver and fired, but Inspector Crane managed to knock the gun low; as it went off the bullet passed between his legs. Bracken stepped backwards and in doing so tripped and fell, but Inspector Crane and Sergeant Aherne managed to hold on to him. However, Bracken managed to fire three more shots, wounding Aherne. As Bracken continued his struggle to escape, he pointed his gun at Head Constable Stuart who managed to deflect it by hitting Bracken on the head, whereupon Stuart received a severe blow in the face from Bracken's gun. After more entanglements with senior officers of the RIC and the mob outside the building, Bracken managed to escape. Volunteers still in the building were arrested. As the police and prisoners left the building, the mob entered and wrecked the furniture and fittings in the hall: 'having wrecked the hall the crowd turned its attention to the band room of the

Volunteers in Charleville Square and carried off the band's instruments and a box of ammunition, but these were afterwards handed over to the police.'[20] The *Irish Times* reported on the injuries suffered by the RIC officers. Inspector Crane received severe bruising to his face; Sergeant Aherne had two bullet wounds to his arm and torso, and was transferred for treatment to Dr Stevens' Hospital in Dublin. The newspaper did not record the injuries suffered by Seamus Brennan at the hands of the mob. Four of the volunteers were charged 'with having feloniously fired at and attacked with intent to murder' the RIC officers.[21] Peadar Bracken went on the run, but remained in Offaly by moving between various safe houses. Seamus Brennan made his way to Dublin and was sent to Larkfield, where he remained until the Rebellion.

While the men at Kimmage did not receive an official announcement about the impending Rebellion, by Holy Week they knew intuitively that it was coming soon. Patrick Pearse had addressed them earlier that week and intimated to them that they would be going into action shortly. He also informed them that they had been appointed an 'official company attached to the Headquarters Battalion of the High Command Staff of the Irish Volunteers'; Arthur Agnew recalled 'we knew there was going to be in a fight, but we did not know when or what it was going to be like'.[22] During that week the food store at Kimmage was cleared out, which suggested to the men that the camp was going to be closed down.

This speculation was further fuelled on Good Friday when five members of the garrison were sent to Kerry to acquire a wireless set. About a week before Good Friday, Michael Collins had discussions with Con Keating and Denis Daly about the possibility of acquiring a wireless system and transmitter from the Wireless College in Cahirciveen. Denis Daly's understanding was that this plot to steal equipment was to enable the volunteers to make wireless contact with a German arms ship (not named in the statement) expected to arrive at Fenit on Easter Sunday. This ship was the *Aud*; it was carrying guns and ammunition for the Volunteers and Roger Casement was on board, but Daly in his statement was very circumspect about naming it.

Apart from Denis Daly, four other volunteers made up the raiding party: Dan Sheehan, Charles Monahan, Colum O'Lochlainn, and Con Keating. Keating was originally from Cahirciveen and had worked for the British Post Office in London; he was a professional wireless operator. Keating believed that 'it might be possible to get the necessary equipment from a wireless college in Cahirciveen that was run by Maurice Fitzgerald'.[23] The school was located within 100 yards of the local RIC Barracks in Cahirciveen and was unoccupied at night. Collins appointed Denis Daly leader of the group; before they left Dublin, they were each given a revolver. On Good Friday, the five men travelled to Killarney by train, where they met Tommy McInerney from Limerick, who owned the two cars that were being used in the venture. His plan was to travel to Cahirciveen via Killorglin, force their way into the wireless college, remove the material they needed and pass it on to a group of the Tralee Volunteers.

The men estimated that they could take the wireless equipment to Tralee on Saturday morning. Keating, Monahan and Sheehan were to remain in Kerry with the equipment, while the other three would return Dublin. The party divided into two groups: Keating, Sheehan, and Monahan travelled with McInerney, while Daly and O'Lochlainn travelled in the second car with the tools. The car in which Daly was travelling led with the agreement that each car would keep within sight of each other. They left as it was getting dark and after about three-quarters of an hour Daly noticed that the second car was not behind them. They stopped and waited, but when the car did not show up they concluded that it must have taken an alternative route. At one point they were stopped by the police and questioned but were let go; after some time waiting at Killorglin they moved on to Cahirciveen. As the other car was still missing, the men reasoned that the police must have stopped it and perhaps arrested the men. Neither Daly nor O'Lochlainn had any experience of wireless and they decided to return to Dublin. On the train, they received news at Mallow of the arrest of Roger Casement.

As for the other car, the driver had inexplicably driven off Ballykissane Pier and the three volunteers – Keating, Sheehan, and Monahan – drowned. The driver managed to escape. While Daly was very circumspect in his witness statement regarding the possibility that the whole thing was connected to the *Aud* and Roger Casement, the report in the *Irish Times* was less so. The report written in the wake of the Rebellion said that car had taken a wrong turn and went over Ballykissane Quay into the River Lane and that the driver, McInerney, escaped but the three volunteers drowned. The newspaper, however, reported that when the bodies were recovered 'on them were found revolvers, ammunition and Sinn Fein badges'.[24] The report went on to link this event with the arrival of the *Aud* in Tralee Bay and the arrest of Roger Casement. Daly remained unaware of the fate of his comrades until Sunday morning, when he read about it in the *Sunday Independent*. The men at Kimmage, preoccupied with the palpable sense that something momentous was pending, were unaware of the accident. When Roger Casement was arrested in Kerry and the arms shipment lost as the ship sank, Eoin McNeill reacted by cancelling the Easter Sunday manoeuvres and the men at Kimmage were left feeling frustrated.

The memories of the individual men on this are interesting. Arthur Agnew said that on Saturday morning they were served 'an extra special breakfast, everyone received two rashers and two sausages', and they were informed that this was the last meal they would eat in Kimmage.[25] John O'Connor said they 'were advised by Captain Plunkett to go to confession that evening and most of us went to Mount Argus, and those of us whose footwear had by now become worn out were given money to buy good marching boots'.[26]

4 Three volunteers: *from left*: Joe Good, John 'Blimey' O'Connor (sitting), and Ernie
Nunan. Courtesy of Cáit Mhic Ionnraic, daughter of John (Blimey) O'Connor

On Easter Sunday morning, George Plunkett gave them permission to attend Mass at nearby Mount Argus. As the men were getting ready for parade the countermanding order arrived and Plunkett then ordered that they should once again be confined to camp. The witness statements clearly convey the gloom that set in after the cancellation order. Arthur Agnew recalled that 'we were "standing to" all day Sunday and nothing further happened, and food was scarce because no rations had been issued'.[27] John McGallogly said that the men spent Sunday in doubts, grumbling and repeating rumours. By this time, they knew they had lost three comrades in Kerry.

However, they did have a pleasant distraction: Geraldine Plunkett and Thomas Dillon were married that morning. She said that 'the Liverpool Lambs gave her a great send off'.[28] Joseph Plunkett and Grace Gifford were also to be married that morning, but according to Geraldine he cancelled the wedding because he was busy with the preparation for the Rebellion.

Meanwhile, on Sunday morning, Peadar Bracken travelled to Dublin from Tullamore to query the countermanding and he was ordered to stay at Kimmage that night. According to his statement, he had an interview with Patrick Pearse, who sent him to see James Connolly, who handed him a commission as captain. That evening Michael Collins visited the garrison and ordered Joseph Gleeson to report to Liberty Hall. When Gleeson got to Liberty Hall he was given a letter for the Kimmage Garrison by James Connolly 'in the presence of Patrick Pearse'.[29] He returned to Kimmage and passed it to Plunkett; this was the Kimmage Garrison's mobilization order.

# 4. The chaos of rebellion

According to Seamus Robinson, on Easter Monday morning George Plunkett, who had a pre-occupied demeanour, suddenly appeared wearing a broad smile and carrying a sword. He ordered the men to parade with full equipment and hard rations. Robinson said that 'fifty-four members of the garrison assembled at about 11.15 a.m. and marched to the tram terminus at Dolphin's Barn'.[1] However, Joseph Gleeson said that it 'was 10.30 a.m. when they left and that they boarded the tram at Harold's Cross'.[2] Robinson also said that they marched out of Larkfield carrying all their arms, which included rifles, shotguns, small arms, crowbars, pickaxes, pikes, and 'French bayonets on broomsticks'.[3] Arthur Agnew's recollection was that 'nearly everyone had a pike, the staffs of which were of various lengths, some of them six feet'.[4] Agnew said that when they boarded the tram 'George Plunkett insisted on paying the conductor our tickets'.[5] John McGallogly recalled:

> We were a unique body of soldiers going into action on a tram. Each man had a different kind of kit. No two had it affixed in the same way and probably no one could have put it on the same way twice.[6]

John O'Connor remembered 'being on the top of the open-deck tram playing national airs on a flute which I had brought with me and the lads joined in singing lustily'.[7] Michael Collins did not march out of Larkfield with the men on Easter Monday; he had been appointed *aide de camp* to Joseph Plunkett and so remained in the city. Some weeks before the rebellion Joseph Plunkett, who was suffering glandular TB, had an operation and was in a nursing home from which he discharged himself. He booked into the Metropole Hotel in Sackville Street, which was located next to the GPO. In her witness statement Geraldine Plunkett Dillon said that on Friday night Michael Collins had brought Joe's bag from the nursing home to the hotel and she, with Collins, spent a half-hour with him.

The men of the Kimmage Garrison left the tram at O'Connell Bridge, formed into two sections under Seamus Brennan and Peadar Bracken, and marched to Liberty Hall with George Plunkett in command. The column of rebels marched down Lower Abbey Street, and Robinson said that it was only when they arrived at Liberty Hall and were met by Margaret Skinnider, who told him, 'it's on', that the men knew that revolution was about to begin.[8] Joe Good recalled seeing Joseph Plunkett standing with plans in his hand outside Liberty Hall:

He was beautifully dressed, having high tan leather boots, spurs, pince-nez and looked like any British brass hat officer. Connolly looked drab beside him in a bottle green thin serge uniform. The form of dress of the two men impressed me as representing two different ideas of freedom.[9]

The Kimmage Garrison, with the Irish Citizen Army, now became the vanguard of the Rebel Army led by the joint leadership of the Irish Citizen Army and the Irish Volunteers. The rank-and-file of this vanguard comprised 194 members of the Irish Citizen Army, the 54 men from Kimmage and Winifred Carney, who was a member of the Belfast branch of Cumann na mBan.[10] The various memories of the men as they left Liberty Hall are interesting; Arthur Agnew recalled that they had a 'lorry load of ammunition, supplies, and a cab', and he believed 'that Thomas Clarke and Séan McDermott were in the cab'.[11] He also observed Michael O'Rahilly – known as The O'Rahilly – arriving in his car. Denis Daly's memory of this episode is that, as they mobilized in front of Liberty Hall, he was put 'in charge of a section of men and ordered to guard the car that was to that carry some of the leaders to the GPO'.[12] Joe Good remembered removing some boxes from Liberty Hall that were loaded onto the car, which he said was 'the total sum of our transport'.[13] Then he said the whole party proceeded to the GPO via Lower Abbey Street with Pearse, Connolly, and Plunkett marching in front, the car behind and then the Irish Citizen Army with the Kimmage Garrison following in the rearguard. Joe Good described the charge at the GPO:

> On arrival at the GPO, George Plunkett gave the order, 'Into line left turn' This brought us into two lines facing the main entrance to the GPO. I heard him then say '"A" section turn right' and "A" section went to Henry Street. Then he said section '"D" left turn'. This brought the section I was in facing O'Connell Bridge I hear George say '"B" and "C" sections charge'. He nearly lost his voice at this time.[14]

Joseph Gleeson and Blimey O'Connor were in the group that charged the GPO; Gleeson said that there was a policeman on duty and that O'Connor took him prisoner. The policeman was Constable Edward Dunphy and he was held prisoner in the GPO until the retreat.

Geraldine Plunkett Dillon and her husband had spent their honeymoon night in the Imperial Hotel across the street from the GPO, and from a balcony window had a view of the events as they unfolded. She said they 'watched the volunteers stopping milk carts and food carts and bringing the food into the GPO'.[15] She also witnessed the volunteers start to make a barricade using a tram. Unable to turn it over, they put a bomb into it but when it failed to go off 'Joe Plunkett came out of the GPO and shot at it with his Mauser from about 30 yards', which exploded the bomb.[16] Geraldine said that Rory O'Conner came over to inform Thomas Dillon that Joe Plunkett had ordered both of them to go 'back to Larkfield to try and get the big tar still running, so that if it should happen that things turned better then was now anticipated the phenol could be used for munitions'.[17]

The men of the Kimmage Garrison were strangers to the city, mainly because they had been kept on a tight rein in Larkfield, and were consequently ignorant of the geography of the city. There had been no organized exercises in reconnaissance for the men and they were never at any point given an outline map of the immediate city centre area. This caused some problems. When the Kimmage Garrison marched towards the GPO, John McGallogly and Joe Duffy were ordered to barricade the houses at the top of Lower Abbey Street and were led to some flats over Kelly's bicycle shop from where they carried out the order. When they were finished, they returned to the street and discovered that the rest of the volunteers had moved on and neither man knew where the GPO was located. However, McGallogly, who had at one time stayed with the Ryan family in Ballybough, decided they would go there and get some help. While in the Ryan's house, they saw a volunteer in uniform pass the window; on catching up with him, they were brought to a field somewhere in Fairview where Diarmuid Lynch was mobilizing two companies of Irish Volunteers. The two men pitched in with this group and while engaged in building a barricade at the junction of Summerhill and Portland Row saw another company of volunteers pass by; on recognizing one of them McGallogly decided to join this group as it made its way to the GPO, where they rejoined their comrades of the Kimmage Garrison.

In the aftermath of the charge at the GPO, the ensuing chaos sometimes bordered on the absurd. The first casualty among the rebel army was Liam Clarke, a member of the St Enda's contingent which had arrived about 15 minutes after vanguard of the rebel army occupied the GPO. Clarke was apparently carrying a grenade in his pocket, and as he climbed through a window at the GPO it exploded when it made contact with the window. He suffered serious facial injuries and lost one eye. He was removed to Jervis Street hospital for treatment and recovered but went on to develop 'a life-long addiction to morphine'.[18]

Amidst the chaos, the Rebel Army raised a flag above the GPO. However, it would appear that there were possibly two flags raised on the GPO that Easter Monday, and there are several claimants for the honour of raising it. The story of the flag – or flags – is an interesting tale and a testimony to the problems created by personal subjectivity and individual memory. According to the account of the Scottish Brigade, when the Kimmage Garrison got to the GPO Patrick Pearse nominated volunteer Paddy Morrin, who was a steeplejack from Glasgow, 'to hoist the flag of the Irish Republic on the flagpole of the GPO'.[19] However, Eamon Bulfin in his witness statement said that there were two flags on the post office. He claimed in his witness statement that he was given one of the flags, which he described it as 'an ordinary Irish Flag, green with the harp and in white letters (inscribed) across the middle were the words Irish Republic'.[20] He could not recollect who gave it to him and 'thought it might have been Willie Pearse'.[21] This description does not fit the flag taken from the GPO. Bulfin said that he raised this flag on the corner of the GPO behind a balustrade on the Princes Street side of the building; he said there were about 20 or 25 men on the roof and that he saw another flag being raised at the same time. He said this flag was hoisted by a member of the Kimmage Garrison, known by the name of Redmond. This was the alias used by Joseph Gleeson, who did not mention this episode in his statement.

Another contender for the raising of the flag is Robert Walpole, who with Theobald Fitzgerald made a joint statement on the issue. Apparently, the impetus for their statement – which deals solely with this issue – was prompted by the obituary of Gearoid O'Sullivan, published in several newspapers in 1948. O'Sullivan, a well-known barrister at law, was in the GPO in 1916 and later became Adjutant General of the Irish Defence Forces. The newspapers and in particular the *Irish Times* gave him the credit for hoisting the flag.

The Walpole/Fitzgerald statement recorded that about 15 minutes after the taking of the post office of James Connolly handed a parcel to Walpole who recalled:

> Some 15 minutes after taking the position, say 12.15 p.m., Commandant General Connolly, who was a friend, said, 'Here is a job for you'. I asked, 'What is it?' 'Take this parcel, it is the flag, put it up.'[22]

Walpole said that on the roof of the GPO he met Sean Hegarty, who offered to help him. Both men took the flag to the flagpole on the Princes Street side of roof. Apparently, Hegarty pulled the flag half way up and Walpole completed the task by pulling it to the top and tying it to the pole. He described this flag: it was 'made of green poplin, on which was painted the words Irish Republic in white and orange letters'.[23] This description fits the flag in the National Museum captured by British Military in the wake of the rebellion. Walpole says that the material of this flag was made of poplin and was woven by Percy Reynolds at Fry's Poplin factory, in Cork Street. Apparently, this flag was painted by Theobald Fitzgerald at the home of Countess de Markievicz, where it hung on the wall of the top back bedroom for a week before the Rebellion. However, Fitzgerald has written in the margin of the witness statement 'my impression is the flag material was bunting'. The flag in the National Museum is made of poplin. Walpole however sowed another seed of doubt when he described the flag as having 'a fringe of gold lace'.[24] The only flag at the GPO that week with a gold lace fringe was the Irish Citizen Army flag. Walpole said James Connolly handed him the flag, and so it is possible that he hoisted the Irish Citizen Army flag on the roof of the GPO. Hayes McCoy, in his book on Irish flags, said that on Wednesday 25 April 'James Connolly dispatched the Irish Citizen Army flag to the Imperial hotel, where it flew until after the surrender'.[25] This suggests that perhaps the Starry Plough Flag hung for almost two days on the GPO alongside the Republican flag carrying the words 'Irish Republic'.

With regard to the role of Gearoid O'Sullivan, Eamon Bulfin said that he did not remember him being there, but added, 'I did not know him at the time though he may have been there'.[26] However, Walpole and Fitzgerald were adamant that he was not present, and 'to their knowledge O'Sullivan was in Cabra on Easter Monday morning and did not arrive at the GPO until the evening'. O'Sullivan said that Liam McGinley of the Glasgow Volunteers and a member of the Kimmage Garrison could back up their story. A reporter with the *Dublin Saturday Post* who observed events in Sackville Street during that week said that on Friday 28 April there was just one flag on the GPO and that it was 'on the Princes Street corner and it was a green flag with the words Irish Republic in white-and-orange letters'.[27]

Meanwhile, the men at the GPO were busy building barricades and getting supplies. Inside the GPO, the men were ordered to fill mailbags with coal from the cellar and place them inside the windows as barricades. At the corner of Sackville Street and Bachelor's Walk, Peadar Bracken and Seamus Robinson blocked access from the bridge to Sackville Street. They began to break into a shop named Hopkins and Hopkins when a DMP man approached them; Cormac Turner held him up at bayonet point, and apparently the police man exclaimed 'don't do that I will go back to barracks those are my instructions if anything happens', so they let him go.[28] They resumed building barricades with furniture, sewing machines and anything from the surrounding buildings they could find. Arthur Agnew said they were joined later that evening by Ned Lawless, Dan Brophy, Jack Kelly, and Peter Caddel form the Fingal Volunteers; they got some sandwiches from the GPO and later 'in the evening some girls from the GPO brought us more sandwich and cakes'.[29] Denis Daly said that when they raided 'a premises on Dame Street for electrical supplies' and later made several trips to Findlater's shop on Sackville Street and several provision shops in the vicinity, they used The O'Rahilly's car to ferry the looted material to the GPO.[30]

On several occasions in the witness statements the shooting of civilians was justified by the claim that the civilians were looting. There are many accounts in the historiography of 'women in shawls' wearing expensive jewellery, fur coats, and other expensive apparel, which veer thinly between entertaining accounts and derision. Looting in Dublin was a fact, but it needs to be examined in the wider context of war and removed from the implicit attitude that suggests that those who looted were somehow not Irish and deserved all they got. Within the historiography of the Rebellion, 'looting' is always ascribed to the general populace, while the taking of food and material by the rebel army is described almost as a patriotic duty.

One of the most common threads in the accounts of all Irish Volunteers and Cumann namBan members who gave statements to the Bureau of Military

History is their fixation with food. The accounts of the participants on the issue of acquiring food are immensely interesting. These accounts were most likely written initially during the 1930s as applications for the War of Independence pension. Reading this material, it is possible to understand the confusion and chaos that existed and to explore the rebels' perceptions on the looting. They make a clear distinction between the looting carried out by the rebels, the British soldiers and the civilians of Dublin. For example, almost without exception the rebels' perception and the subsequent historiography suggests that the rebels commandeered food, the British army simply took food, and without exception the civilians looted food.

When the rebellion began, the rebel army had some rations but extra food was necessary. They solved the problem by looting local shops and hotels in the immediate vicinity of their respective garrisons. The garrison at the GPO had plenty of food because the men looted food from Findlater's provisions shop in Sackville Street, where they left a receipt signed on behalf of the Provisional Government. There were several hotels in Sackville Street and the rebels also took advantage of their stores. May McLoughlin, a Clann na Gael girl scout, recalled that there was plenty of food in the GPO and that when she 'was ordered to go to the kitchen and rest she saw for the first time in her life a whole salmon cooked laid in a dish'.[31] The shops in Moore Street were also the source of much this food. Eilis Ni Riain recalled that 'for the first few days they helped in the kitchen where the Volunteers kept them supplied with food commandeered from various shops'.[32] They took 'ham, tomatoes, tea, and sugar and milk'; she also recalled that for the first time in her life she 'sampled some tomatoes and sugarless tea'.[33] One of the men particularly good at commandeering food for the garrison was nicknamed 'Looter Flood' by his comrades. Essentially, the rebel army had removed the best of the food in the city centre before citizens got going.

Cumann na mBan were active in Sackville Street, reacting in part to Pearse's appeal that there was 'work for everyone, for the men in the fighting line and for the women in the provision of food and first-aid'.[34] The members of Cumann na mBan rallied to this call and they moved from building to building in search of volunteers, organizing first-aid stations and procuring food. Brigid Martin said that with other women she had reported for duty to Captain Weafer in Sackville Street, who sent them to Clery's Shop, where they took 'aprons, sheets, towels, soaps, dishcloths' and anything they could use to set up a 'a first-aid station at 14 Lower Sackville Street'.[35]

By Monday night and Tuesday morning, the local citizenry had joined in the looting and Patrick Pearse sent some of the volunteers to disperse them. Peadar Bracken, who was in Hopkins and Hopkins, said he 'held up several looters from the window and compelled them to abandon what they were taking'.[36] It is clear from the witness statements that looting for personal gain by citizens was unacceptable to the rebel army and that they were ruthless in stopping it. Commandant W.J. Brennan Whitmore was the officer commanding the volunteer position on North Earl Street; on Monday evening he began organizing the building of barricades in Sackville Street. He led his men into the Pillar café where they began to throw all the furniture into the street to create a barricade when he saw 'a "shawlie" a big buxom young woman who yelled to her companion "look they are throwing out the lovely furniture" and she seized the armchair and started to carry it off'; he said 'once this got started it would be farewell to my barricade' and 'there is nothing more lawless and irresponsible than a crowd that has got out of hand'.[37] Apparently, up to this point the crowd in the street was very well behaved. Brennan Whitmore, unhappy with this development, said 'as soon as the furniture hit the street the natural cupidity of human flesh flared and it was certain it would spread' and at the point of his automatic pistol he ordered the 'shawlie' to leave the chair back on the barricade, and she very sensibility complied.[38]

When the rebellion began, there was wholesale looting of both food and non-food shops in the immediate vicinity of Sackville Street, Grafton Street and other main shopping areas. James Stephens said that 'by Tuesday the favourite shops targeted for looting were mainly haberdashers, shoe shops, and sweet shops' and the children 'were having the sole gorge of their lives and until they die the insurrection of 1916 will have a sweet savour for them'.[39]

However, this sugar rush was short-lived, as rebels and British soldiers alike fired on looters. As the week wore on, those families imprisoned within their homes faced the misery of being without food. Stephens said that by Friday there was no bread or milk; one young girl told him that her family and another family who took refuge in her home 'had not eaten for three days'.[40] On the fourth day, her father had managed to acquire two loaves of bread, which he divided between fourteen adults and children. In several areas, basic food was unavailable and in many localities children, especially infants, suffered severely, while some bakers who managed to continue production raised their prices. With the Post Offices and banks all closed people could not get access to money to buy food, even at the inflated prices. Some of the convents in the city distributed free bread.

Confined as they were to the Larkfield Camp, the men of the Kimmage Garrison had no connection with Cumann na mBan until the rebellion. They had learned the skills of self-sufficiency at Larkfield and they had no problem in looking after their own needs. Brigid Martin recollected watching the men of the Kimmage Garrison in the GPO making 'ammunition from the lead they had taken from the *Freeman's Journal*, while simultaneously feeding big sides of looted beef into the ovens for lunch'.[41]

On Wednesday 26 April, the British had brought the gunship *Helga* up the Liffey and the bombardment of the city centre began. By this time, the men of the GPO garrison were spending much of their time avoiding sniper fire, having effectively placed themselves in a siege situation. By Friday 28 April, it became obvious to the rebel army that retreat from the GPO was inevitable.

# 5. Retreat and surrender

By 5 p.m. on Thursday 27 April the 4th Leinsters, the 2/6th Sherwood Foresters, the 3rd Royal Regiment, and the Ulster Composite Battalion under the command of Colonel Portal formed a cordon around the rebels in the Sackville Street area.[1] The reporter for the *Dublin Saturday Post* observing the scene in Sackville Street described the military as 'passively active as British soldiers creep in two and threes over O'Connell Bridge and reconnoitre in the laneways and by-ways in the vicinity'.[2] By Friday, two days after the gunboat *Helga* began bombarding the city centre, additional gunfire rendered Sackville Street a mass of burning buildings. The GPO building now came under direct attack; the *Dublin Saturday Post* described the situation:

> At 4.20 p.m., a field gun barks in the direction of Earl Street. And a column of smoke rose from the upper part of the GPO. Another bang and the column of smoke is augmented ... about 4.45 the dimensions of the column of smoke rising from the GPO assumed dangerously large proportions ... some Sinn Féiners on the roof with a hose trying to cope with the onslaught of the flames. At frequent intervals their frantic efforts to overcome the fire demons are interrupted by ill-directed fire from a maxim gun.[3]

Eamon Bulfin, who was one of the volunteers on the roof, said that at first the hoses worked fine, but that after a while the water ran out. In the GPO, a decision was taken to move the ammunition and explosives down to the cellar. John McGallogly said that the prisoners were used to help move the store of ammunition and explosives to the basement of the building, and that 'the volunteer in charge of the store told me there were 33,000 rounds on hand and there was also some long-range miniature stuff'.[4]

Inside the GPO, there was also a realization that the building would have to be evacuated. The previous day, members of Cumann na mBan were asked to leave the building, but when they refused were allowed to stay. However, as the GPO came under direct attack the necessity of evacuating the building was clear and the women left the building in two separate groups. Gertie Colley recalled that Desmond Fitzgerald took her aside and Pearse gave her a large Red Cross flag attached to a flagpole. He ordered her, with Bridie Connolly, to lead the other women up Henry Street to Jervis St. Hospital and seek admission there. The second group left through the back of the building; they too were directed to go to the hospital. This group also used a Red Cross

5. Map of Moore Street and Henry Place. Courtesy of Trinity College map library and the Land Valuation Office, Dublin.

flag, affording them protection, and they accompanied a number of wounded volunteers. Winifred Carney, Julia Grennan, and Elizabeth O'Farrell remained in the GPO with the men.

Joe Good said that as dusk was setting the GPO was burning fiercely from the roof to the ground floor, with the rebels still in the process of evacuation. The exit door was narrow, and as the volunteers rushed to leave the GPO there was a crush at the doorway; some guns were accidently discharged, wounding several of the rebels. The door from which they emerged was directly in line with Henry Place and they crossed to this laneway.

The main group of the rebels and leaders retreated to Henry Place, sending their prisoners out first. Eamon Bulfin said that 'because it was dusk they could not see very well', that it was chaotic and 'it was every man for himself'.[5] As they entered Henry Place, Jack Plunkett said that they 'were very thirsty and some of the men broke into the mineral water factory'.[6] This factory was located in numbers 2 to 8 Henry Place and was owned by Michael O'Brien. Henry Place was an L-shaped lane; around the bend in the lane there was a right-angle turn into Moore Lane and the street directly facing it was Moore Place. There were five tenement houses in this laneway with several families trapped inside. On the corner of this lane were two tenement houses; these were numbers 9 and 10 Henry Place, and the latter was a detached building.

When the volunteers reached this area they had a problem getting past what most of the men describe as a white house. It was dark at this time, and the only light came from the inferno in Sackville Street. Joe Good believed they were coming under fire from a group of rebels inside the building and recollected that 'there were shouts of, you are firing on your own men, from our party, but the firing persisted'.[7] According to Arthur Agnew, 'an attempt was made to storm the house but it was discovered in the nick of time that it was not occupied and that it was the ricochets off the wall gave the impression that fire was coming from there'.[8] The retreat came to a halt at this point as chaos reigned, but they managed to cross the bottom of Moore Lane in twos and threes and they groped about in the dark laneway for another building and safety. Constable Edward Dunphy was wounded in the hand as he ran across this laneway. Good said that 'some volunteers attempted to break down a large door with their rifle butts' and inadvertently 'shot three or four men who were behind them'.[9] At this point, they were close to 11, 12, and 13 Henry Place, which was the stable and loft belonging to Michael O'Brien's mineral water company. Joe Good said that they put 'James Connolly down in the middle of the road and he shouted out what seemed to be orders'.[10] The men then entered a building and brought out a cart/dray to build a barricade at the bottom of Moore Lane. Good said the men then made it to the corner house at (10) Moore Street.

According to the statements of the men of the Kimmage Garrison, it was at this point that The O'Rahilly decided to charge the British army barricade at the top of Moore Street. Joe Good 'heard The O'Rahilly calling for 20 men with bayonets to make a charge'.[11] Good said he said that he personally could not figure out from their location what exactly The O'Rahilly wanted to charge, because from their position in the laneway it was not possible to see the top end of Moore Street. Good said that O'Rahilly then began shouting at them 'are you Irishmen that you won't charge' and then according to Good 'about 20 men stepped forward'.[12] Apparently, O'Rahilly was trying to reach the confectionery factory Williams and Woods; like the men of the Kimmage Garrison he appeared to be equally ignorant of the geography of this part of the city, as there were alternative routes to this building through the several laneways and back alleys in the area. Instead, he launched a full-frontal charge in an act of bravado for which he paid the ultimate price.

In their witness statements the men of the Kimmage Garrison describe this particular event. Denis Daly said that O'Rahilly left Henry Place and went back to Henry Street, from where he planned to launch his charge. He said that O'Rahilly took charge of a group of about 40 rebels and divided them into two groups of 20 so that each group would work its way up either side of Moore Street, but Jack Plunkett said it was 11 men. Joe Good said that the men led by The O'Rahilly was bereft of bayonets 'but that one man was armed with a shotgun, and a bayonet of one-inch by three-and-one-sixteenth-inches of Bessemer steel, a number of these bayonets were made at Kimmage, but they would have bent against three-ply wood'.[13] As soon as the men entered Moore Street, they came under heavy fire from the British army at the top of the street. Daly said that everyone in front of him was shot, including O'Rahilly. Daly took refuge with some of the other men in a doorway about 100 yards from the British position and they decided to try to move back towards the GPO. They made it to Coles Lane where they reached the safety of the cellar of a grocery and wine shop that fronted onto Henry Street. There they discovered men, women and children taking refuge, and the volunteers remained there with them until the surrender.

Meanwhile, having blocked the entrance to Moore Lane and getting a little respite, Joe Good calculated that in getting past this point between 18 and 20 rebels were injured and there were several civilian causalities. The men of the Kimmage Garrison did not shy away from talking about the effect of the rebellion on the civilians who suffered in the retreat from the GPO.

At one point in Henry Place Joe Good said he 'heard one of the men shout "stand clear" and then burst the lock of a door with a shot or shots', and unfortunately a girl and her father were trying to open the door. Both were hit, she fatally.[14] This victim was Brigid McKane, who was 15-years old; she received a fatal gunshot wound to her head and died instantly. Her death certificate records her address as 10 Henry Place. A second child who died in the retreat from the GPO was William Mullen who was 9-years old and lived in Moore Place; he died in his home from a 'gunshot wound in thorax'.[15]

When Joe Good entered number 10 Henry Place (where Brigid McKane was shot) he said there was a 'Red Cross man' with him and when he saw a piece of her skull on the ground he 'slipped it into his coat pocket so that no one would discover it'. He described it, saying it was 'about the size of an orange; it was clean and white as I imagined a baby's would be'.[16] Sean McDermott apologized profusely to the family, and promised that there would be an inquiry into the incident.

Meanwhile Patrick Pearse, who was last to leave the GPO, was accompanied by Seamus ua Coamhanaigh. The latter said they both 'walked quietly across Henry Street and into Henry Place'.[17] He identified the Red Cross man as Seamus Donegan and a member of the Kimmage Garrison. Donegan told him about Brigid, and he said that 'when he was informed that there was a girl in a room who had been shot, he groped around in the darkness to find out what was wrong with her'.[18] He thought he had put his fingers into her mouth, because he thought he felt her teeth, but when he struck a match, he found that he had put his fingers through a hole in her skull. In the same house ua Coamhanaigh stumbled across John King of the Liverpool volunteers who he said 'got a bullet in his hip and was lying on the floor bleeding and I suppose partly unconscious, being kicked and trampled on by passing men'.[19] He gave him assistance and bandaged him up and he survived.

Seamus ua Coamhanaigh said he continued on his way and followed the first batch of retreating rebels as they moved up Moore Street by breaking holes through the walls of buildings. As they groped their way through the buildings, they burst into living rooms and bedrooms where terrified people were huddled together in total darkness wondering what would happen to them, and ua Coamhanaigh said he 'felt very sorry for them because' the rebels were 'bringing them death and destruction'.[20]

In Sackville Street, the reporter for the *Dublin Saturday Post* was still observing the situation and his report explains the mystery of how the republican flag survived the firestorm at the GPO. It stated:

> High above the building the Republican flag flutters excitedly over the stifling atmosphere of dust laden smoke … With the aid of a powerful field glass I see its white letters with the words 'Irish republic' … At nine o'clock the GPO is reduced to ruins. Its four granite walls look like the bones of a skeleton skull. Its core is nothing but smouldering debris. The fluttering of the flag grows feebler. In the dimness of the night, I see it give an occasional flicker as if revived by a gust of air. At length at 9.51 p.m., the staff supporting it begins to waver and in a second falls out towards the street.[21]

The flagpole fell to the street and the flag survived the battle. This flag was taken by the British soldiers and is now held in the National Museum at Collins Barracks.

Meanwhile, the vanguard of the rebel army had burrowed their way from numbers 10 to 25 Moore Street and Eamon Bulfin said:

> We spent Friday night barricading all the houses that we occupied by throwing down all the furniture from the rooms – clearing all the rooms – down the stairways into the bottom halls and blocking up the doorways … We had to evacuate the civilians from the houses, of course, under great pressure, too some were trying to cross the street.[22]

Moore Street was a veritable no man's land at this point and in the darkness both sides appeared to be shooting at any kind of movement. Subsequently some civilians were shot, and John O'Connor said he saw some of them 'killed by the enemy while attempting to cross Moore Street'.[23] O'Connor said that 'at about 3 a.m. on Saturday morning the fire in the GPO reached the explosives in the cellar and the resultant explosion was terrific'.[24]

Early Saturday morning some of the men decided to emulate The O'Rahilly's charge towards the British army barricade at the top of Moore Street. Peadar Bracken with Harry Boland and J.J. Walsh organized men with rifles and bayonets for the attack and Eamonn Bulfin said it was decided that 'George Plunkett should take command'.[25] Peadar Bracken said 'they sent a dispatch back to headquarters at about 2 p.m., but they were told that a truce was in progress'.[26] The fact that headquarters was just nine building down the street and Elizabeth O'Farrell had already walked up Moore Street at 12.34 p.m. carrying a white flag illustrates the confusion within the rebel army at this point. Regarding the aborted attack on the British barricade, Seamus ua Coamhanaigh, who was one of the group, said 'it was lucky it was called off because we would all have been killed long before we reached the barricade, and in any case none of us knew anything about bayonet fighting'.[27]

SURRENDER

The end came when Elizabeth O'Farrell was sent up Moore Street with an oral message of surrender. Sean McDermott ordered her to procure a white flag, which he then hung out of a window to ensure that the British soldiers would not fire on her. O'Farrell left the building at about 12.45 p.m., carrying the flag and wearing her nurse's uniform with the Red Cross insignia on her front apron and arm. She walked along Moore Street towards the army post and on reaching it informed the officer that she 'brought a verbal message from Pearse to the commander of the British Forces to the effect that he (Commandant Pearse) would like to treat with him'.[28] He ordered that the Red Cross insignia be cut from her clothes and she was searched 'in case she was a spy'.[29] At this point, she was deemed a prisoner, and was held for about an hour until Brigadier General Lowe arrived.

O'Farrell repeated the message of surrender to Lowe, and he responded by ordering her to return to Pearse and inform him that General Lowe would not 'treat with him until he made an unconditional surrender', adding that 'if she did not return within the half-hour hostilities must continue'.[30] A written note to this effect was given to her to pass onto to Pearse and then she walked up Moore Street and passed the written and verbal message to Pearse. The note read,

> To Patrick Pearse; 29 April 1916, 4.40 p.m.
> A woman has come in and tells me you wish to negotiate with me. I am prepared to receive you in Britain Street at the north end, provided that you surrender unconditionally. You will proceed up Moore Street accompanied by the woman who brings you this note, under a white flag.[31]

The leaders of the rebel army discussed the situation, and O'Farrell was sent back up Moore Street with their reply. O'Farrell did not know what was in the note. General Lowe read it, and again sent her back to Pearse with the verbal message that if she did not return accompanied by Pearse with Connolly on a stretcher, hostilities would be resumed. After receiving this message, Pearse, accompanied by O'Farrell, walked up the street where he surrendered to General Lowe. For the fourth time that day, O'Farrell walked back down Moore Street to the garrison, carrying written instructions on how to surrender.

In her account of the time just before the surrender at Moore Street, Julia Grennan recalled that a number of the men gathered in the back drawing room and knelt to say the Rosary: 'This picture will never fade from my memory and they knelt holding the rifles they so soon were to surrender in their left hands, the beads in the other'.[32]

The surrender was agreed on Saturday afternoon, and as instructed the rebels brought out the wounded and left them in the middle of the street. Joe Good said that James Connolly was carried out first by four of the men. He said these volunteers had washed, shaved, and polished as if for a parade. He said that before Connolly was taken from the building he sat up in bed, and Winifred Carney held a hand mirror across his body as he shaved himself with a cut-throat razor. Good, who was sitting on the bed, noticed that Joseph Plunkett had lost one of his spurs and on pointing this out to him Plunkett kicked the spur under the bed. Then they carried the rest of the wounded out into Moore Street. There were a number of British soldiers among this group.

Around 4.40 p.m. the fire brigade was allowed into Sackville Street. They set up 'two pumping engines on O'Connell Bridge' and laid a line of hose 'along the footpaths towards Middle Abbey Street'.[33] The first civilian non-combatant to be allowed to enter Sackville Street was Fr Brendan O'Brien

ODC and he was accompanied by a military escort. There was the body of an old man near the bridge, and as the priest 'administered to him the soldiers by his side removed their hats as he imparted his benediction'.[34] At this point in Moore Street, the Red Cross Voluntary Aid Detachments units moved in, organized first-aid stations and moved through the buildings searching for the civilian dead and wounded.

The rebels were then lined up and marched under a white flag back down Moore Street into Sackville Street, where they laid down their arms opposite the Gresham Hotel near the Parnell monument. The rebels from the Four Courts were also brought to Sackville Street for their formal surrender and laid down their arms in the same place. John Shouldice, who was with this group, said when he first saw the devastation in the street:

> The appearance of Sackville Street and the GPO – what was left of it – was an unforgettable sight. From the GPO to O'Connell Bridge on both sides of the street the buildings were mostly burned out ... The bodies of some civilians shot during the week were lying about also a few horses about O'Connell Bridge. The heart of the city presented a picture of utter desolation.[35]

The guns of the rebel army were gathered and taken to the British army ordnance stores at Islandbridge, where they were simply placed in a room. In the immediate aftermath of the Rebellion, the British army raided several homes in the Dublin area and removed 360 legally held guns. These were put with the rebels' guns, but no one labelled them in order to distinguish them from the rebels' hardware. Into this chaos came the souvenir hunters. Within days, the officer in charge of the depot received several requests for some of the guns. In early May, the Commandant of the Royal Irish Constabulary depot in Dublin, Edward H. Pearson, asked for some of the guns. On 5 May, a letter was received from Prince Alexander of Battenberg requesting one of the 'Mauser rifles and a specimen of an old Irish pike', and 'on behalf of King George V' he asked that he be allowed 'to select some unspecified items'.[36] Lieutenant Colonel Decies of the Military Headquarters Staff gave permission and said that all other applicants would have to wait until the two Royals had made their decisions. On 10 May, the depot received a request from the registrar of the College of Surgeons, who asked for some of the rifles and bayonets belonging to the rebels who held the college. He also assured the military that 'comparatively little malicious damage had been done in the college'.[37] On 12 May, the Assistant Director of Ordnance informed the Registrar of the College of Surgeons that he could send a representative to the ordnance depot and take his choice from a small quantity of rifles and bayonets that had been set aside for them.

Meanwhile the owners of the 360 guns seized by the military sought the return of their property. The authorities gave permission for the return of 310 guns on the basis that the owners were loyal citizens. Fifty applicants were refused due to their suspected loyalty. As the successful 310 applicants turned up to collect their guns, a problem was uncovered. Sixty of the guns were missing because apparently they had given to the souvenir hunters. Major General W. Fry, the officer in charge, made a request that the owners be given monetary compensation for their loss. Consequently, all the guns on display in various museums and sold in the trade of 1916 memorabilia, cannot with certainty be described as a gun actually used by the rebels.

After the completion of the surrender, retribution was swift, as over a period of ten days the leaders of the rebellion were court-martialled and executed by firing squad at Kilmainham Goal. The execution of Joseph Plunkett took place on 4 May, the day after he was married to Grace Gifford in the chapel at Kilmainham by the Revd Father McCarthy of the Priory of St James. That evening Grace returned to the prison to visit her new husband for ten minutes in the company of a guard, and this was the last time they met. The other two Plunkett brothers, George and Jack, were sentenced to penal servitude for life. With regard to the rest of the Kimmage Garrison, because the men used aliases it can be difficult to trace what happened to them after the rebellion. Those men recorded in the statements received sentences that ranged from penal servitude to internment without trial.

John McGallogly said that he was court-martialled, along with Sean McGarry, J.J. Walsh, and Willie Pearse, with the latter two in uniform. McGallogly said Lieutenant King, whom he had taken prisoner Princes Street, gave evidence against him and said that he had 'seen the other three in the GPO'.[38] Intent on hiding their Scottish accents, McGallogly and Sean McGarry remained silent throughout. McGallogly and his brother used the name Doherty as an alias. The *Irish Times* reported that John McGallogly/Doherty was tried on the same day as J.J Walsh and Willie Pearse.

J.J. Walsh told the court he had no official position in the Volunteers and Willie Pearse explained he was merely a personal attaché of his brother. However, Willie Pearse was not a passive participant in the preparation for rebellion. Apart from making the moulds for bombs at St Enda's, he was Captain of the Rathfarnham Company of the Irish Volunteers, and on 21 April 1916 he sent out mobilization orders that he signed as 'Captain and Acting Chief of Staff'.[39]

McGallogly said that immediately after the courts martial, the men were moved with 18 others to Kilmainham Gaol while the courts martial decided on their fate. He said that during the early hours of the following morning, a British army officer came to his cell to inform him of the sentence. McGallogly recalled that the officer said:

You have been tried, found guilty and sentenced to death. Do you understand? I said yes. He paused a second or two and then continued, out of consideration of mercy the sentence has been commuted to penal servitude for ten years. Do you understand? Again, I said yes. He told the others to shake me and I was duly shaken.[40]

Jack Plunkett described his trial and sentencing almost in the same way. McGallogly speculated that the officer 'ordered him to be shaken because of his lack of reaction to the death sentence.'[41] The officer then asked McGallogly if he wanted anything to eat, and gave him three army ration biscuits, after which he fell asleep and did not hear the executions. Arthur Agnew, Alex Carpenter, Michael Collins, Denis Daly, Bernard Friel, John Gleeson (alias Redmond) and Joe Good were all interned without trial.

In a handwritten statement about the members of the Glasgow Volunteers, Joe Robinson mentioned by name some men of the Kimmage Garrison not mentioned in his brother's list. This problem might have arisen due to the use of aliases; he added the names of Francis and Michael Flanagan to the list. He also mentioned a man known simply as McGinley, whose home address was given as New York City. This man was apparently a member of the 'A' Company Glasgow Irish Volunteers; sent to Dublin before the rebellion, he settled at Kimmage as a member of the garrison.

Meanwhile Count and Countess Plunkett did not escape the long arm of law or the military authorities. On 1 May 1916, Inspector McFeely of the DMP arrested Count Plunkett at his residence 26 Upper Fitzwilliam Street and transferred him to military custody. He was arrested because when the police raided his home in Fitzwilliam Street they discovered a complete first-aid dressing station containing 'surgical appliances, lint, bandages, and antiseptic dressing'.[42] There was no direct evidence against the Count except that he lived at Larkfield while it was being used 'as a munitions manufacturing depot and training ground'.[43] As the registered owner of Larkfield, Countess Plunkett was considered equally culpable and arrested some days later. The couple remained in Mountjoy until 10 June 1916, and were then deported to Oxford under section 14e of the Defence of the Realm Act. If they had refused to comply with the order, they would have remained in Mountjoy Jail indefinitely. On 15 June 1916 they signed a document agreeing that if they were liberated from custody they would 'proceed quietly to Oxford and take up residence'.[44]

# 6. The Larkfield Chemical Company and the British Authorities

On 3 May 1916, a detachment of soldiers from the Regiment of the Sherwood Foresters searched Larkfield House and Mill. Geraldine Plunkett Dillon said they ransacked the premises, emptied files onto the floor and removed anything of value – including bedclothes and clothing – but she managed to hide some gun cotton. Thomas Dillon complained that the soldiers removed a typewriter, the contents of the petty cash box and damaged a pressure gauge and a thermometer. He also accused the soldiers of releasing 50 gallons of crude phenol from a still. In a letter of complaint to the authorities he demanded £88 8s.10d. in compensation for damage and loss to his property. The Undersecretary, Sir Matthew Nathan, refused to entertain the claim.

In investigating the company, the authorities discovered many interesting facts about the Larkfield Chemical Company. The vacuum still for distilling crude phenol ordered from Blair Campbell and Company in Glasgow had arrived in early 1916. It was in the process of being installed by a chemical engineer when the rebellion began. On his return to Scotland, the engineer told his employers that he believed Dillon and O'Connor were manufacturing phenol for high explosives, because he saw nitrating pots, and a military book on high explosives at Larkfield, and that 'the Larkfield Chemical Company and the Sinn Féiners shared the same office'.[1] Dillon began to pursue the Scottish company to have the installation completed and threatened them with legal proceedings, and intimated that with his business partner Rory O'Connor, he 'would be seeking damages'.[2] The company ignored him and the managing director David Blair passed the correspondence on to the Ministry of Munitions of War in London, and suggested that the plant might be useful to them.

Thomas Dillon and Rory O'Connor were determined to get some compensation and they made an application to the Property Losses (Committee), Dublin 1916 to try to get some funds. This committee was created to enable 'property owners to claim for damages caused during the Disturbances on 24 April 1916'.[3] In addition, the Larkfield Chemical Company did not have any insurance, so its survival now depended on them getting some compensation. Dillon and O'Connor made a claim on the basis that the soldiers had looted Larkfield. In July, they were informed that their claim could not be entertained. By this time, Thomas Dillon's financial position had become precarious. He was a lecturer in UCD and Geraldine Plunkett Dillon said his salary (£12 10s. a month) was stopped for two months by the president of UCD, Dr Denis Coffey. According to Geraldine, this came about after 'Professor Hugh Ryan had asked Dillon if "he could have been making bombs and he said he could" and his salary was withheld until he said that he had "nothing to do with the Rising"'.[4]

At this point, the Larkfield Chemical Company became central to an investigation involving the Ministry of Munitions of War in Whitehall, London, and the Director of Munitions in Ireland. In late August 1916, Eamon Phipps of the Ministry of War wrote to Sir Matthew Nathan and informed him 'that he could appoint an inspector to visit the Larkfield works and explore the nature of the company, plant, and business'.[5] Phipps' purpose was to ascertain whether the Larkfield Chemical Company could manufacture explosives and if this was the case, a requisition order should be instigated. The man appointed to the task was Mr Andrew Charles Woolmer. On 8 September 1916, he inspected the premises, accompanied at all times by Rory O'Connor. Woolmer said in his final report that:

> The machinery and plant consist of a new 300-gallon phenol still … a Crossly gas engine, gas holder, a Vertical Marshall boiler, vacuum pump, a small five-gallon rectifying still and some other odds and ends, bins and receptacles, tools etc. The … still had been used formerly to treat crude phenol.[6]

Woolmer also reported that the stock of chemicals on the premises consisted of 250 gallons of crude phenol, five-to-six cwt of caustic soda, some French chalk and a small quantity of phenol in pots. In the course of the inspection O'Connor apparently informed the inspector that they were planning to manufacture salicylic acid, but 'it was in its early experimentation'.[7] At this time, salicylic acid was a common ingredient in the treatment of acne, but Woolmer said he did not see any evidence of the production of this acid. In addition, he said that when he checked the company's books he found that the company had purchased 2,000 gallons of crude phenol in February 1916 from the Dublin Tar Company (but returned 1,666 gallons). In March, they purchased another 334 gallons and in May 1916 a further 50 gallons. Woolmer also said that the company had no customers on its books and when he inspected the premises the vacuum still had been dismantled, but he qualified this by saying it had never worked properly and that in its current state it was useless.

On the question of the manufacture of explosives, the inspector said that he did not see any evidence that 'the works have ever been used for the manufacture of explosives' and that when he was conducting the inspection there was no 'apparatus on the premises that would enable this kind of production to take place'.[8] Woolmer said that Rory O'Connor told him that he was aware that suspicion rested on the works, and that when the premises were raided by the military at the time of the rebellion the soldiers had removed certain items. The inspector went on to say that 'if any explosives had ever been made at Larkfield that all evidence had since been removed and in his opinion confiscation of the plant and the material therein would not be a worthwhile exercise'.[9] He also pointed out that if the company attempted to manufacture salicylic acid the Ministry could simply refuse to grant them a licence for the necessary raw material. On examining Woolmer's report, the Ministry of Munitions decided not to take any further any action regarding the Larkfield Chemical Company.

In October 1916, Dillon and O'Connor continued to press for compensation, but were informed by the Property Losses Committee that their claim 'could not be entertained because, it would not make any grant to people in respect of the property of persons suspected of complicity with the outbreak'.[10] This was effectually the end of the road for the Larkfield Chemical Company and the building and machinery therein was abandoned.

Meanwhile, Grace Gifford Plunkett was in occupation at Larkfield House. She was apparently homeless and Geraldine Plunkett Dillon allowed her to stay there. She was still living at Larkfield in September 1916 when she instigated a correspondence with the military authorities seeking a passport to enable her to travel to the USA. In a series of letters, and in her witness statement to the Bureau of Military History, Grace explained how she came to marry that day. In her witness statement, she said that she became engaged to Plunkett on 2 December 1915, but that they did not have immediate plans to marry. She said that she 'was not involved in the nationalist movement' and while Joseph Plunkett had been keen to marry during Lent, she demurred because she was 'on the point of becoming a Catholic' and thought this would be 'a fearful thing to do'.[11] During Easter week, Plunkett managed to send her two notes, and she said that in these notes he explained his sudden keenness to marry. She had been 'thrown out of her home' and he believed that if they married and anything happened to him, 'she would be looked after'.[12] However, in another statement to the Bureau of Military History she said that 'Joe wanted them to marry so they could go into the Rising together'.[13]

Geraldine Plunkett Dillon in her memoir said there was a lot of gossip around Dublin that speculated whether Grace was pregnant. This aspect of the story of this marriage is not considered within the historiography of 1916, where it is presented as a romantic story of thwarted young love, almost like a 1916 Republican version of the legendry lovers Tristan and Isolde. The reality appears to have been much more prosaic. Geraldine said that one day when she visited Grace at Larkfield she went into Grace's bedroom and that she saw 'a large white chamber pot full of blood and a foetus'.[14] At a time when the unwed mother was a social pariah, especially within middle class society, the hasty marriage in Kilmainham Goal makes sense.

Meanwhile, Count and Countess Plunkett had begun a systematic campaign to have their deportation rescinded. The Count at the time of his arrest was Director of the National Museum in Dublin, a position held within the remit of the Department of Agriculture and Technical Instruction for Ireland. In late June 1916, the vice-president G.F. Russell suspended Plunkett, but he was not singled out for special treatment. In the wake of the Rebellion five other civil servants in the Department of Agriculture were suspended for complicity in the Rebellion.[15] Count Plunkett maintained his innocence and in a letter to the secretary of the Museums Association E.E. Lowe, said that he had been deported with his wife without being tried by any court because there was insufficient evidence. He said:

> We are kept out of Ireland lest our very presence there, as the parents of young men so tragically connected with the insurrection, should stir the public feeling to a degree, that the military ... and now because of public events in which I took no part I am forced to look for employment among people who are likely to misunderstand the circumstances of the case ... my nine years of public service should count for something.[16]

Lowe ignored Plunkett's letter and passed it on to the Chief Commissioner of the DMP, Lt. Col. W. Edgeworth Johnstone.

In December 1916, there was a general release of internees and it appeared that the Plunketts had a good case for release. However, Johnstone thought otherwise and he advised the Assistant Undersecretary of State, Sir E. O'Farrell, to keep them in Oxford. He held the opinion that while the Count was relatively harmless as an organizer and leader, 'the countess was the more dangerous of the two, and being a better class then most Sinn Féiners they would draw together the literary and artistic element among the rebels, which are really the most dangerous'.[17]

Within weeks, there was a change of perspective when on 15 January 1917 the Home Office decided 'there were insufficient grounds for excluding Count and Countess Plunkett from the general release of the internees'.[18] On 12 February, Countess Plunkett arrived back in Dublin and the Dublin Metropolitan Police (DMP) observed that she was met 'by about fifty ladies who gave her three cheers, as she drove away in a cab (no. 192), towards her residence, and several of the ladies wore Sinn Féin badges and Rosettes'.[19]

In February 1917, Count Plunkett turned to national politics and put himself forward as a candidate in a by-election in North Roscommon. Technically an independent, Plunkett received support from Sinn Féin and other Republicans and Nationalists. He won the election 3,022 votes against

1,708, but then refused to take his seat in the parliament at Westminster. Instead, he organized a conference of republican and nationalist organizations at the Mansion House in Dublin, on 19 April 1917.

The meeting, billed as an 'Irish Assembly', was not a harmonious event. Count Plunkett presided at the assembly, but instead of negotiating with the growing Sinn Féin organization, he launched a new organization, the 'Liberty League'. After a very heated debate, and as Michael Laffan said 'a split in the classic Irish tradition', the assembly came to an agreement to form a composite committee of nine people from the various groups at the meeting.[20] The members of this committee were Count George Plunkett and his wife Countess Josephine Mary Plunkett representing the Liberty League, Fr Michael O'Flanagan, Cathal Brugha, Dr Thomas Dillon and William O'Brien of the United Irish League (UIL), and Thomas Kelly, Arthur Griffith and Séan Milroy for Sinn Féin. While Count and Countess Plunkett were busy building a new political career, the Larkfield Mill was empty and padlocked.

Sometime in late 1917 Geraldine Plunkett Dillon, now acting as her mother's agent, rented Larkfield House to Mr J. Taylor, a civil servant whom the DMP deemed to be a loyal subject. James O'Neill, the Plunkett family caretaker, was still living in the cottage with a lodger named as Mr Taaffe. The DMP maintained surveillance on the Larkfield complex and on 26 January 1918, Superintendant Owen Brien reported that about 200 Sinn Féin Volunteers had taken over possession of the Hall and were once again drilling and he believed that 'if the situation was allowed to continue it would undoubtedly lead to further mischief'.[21] He was also of the opinion that Countess Plunkett had given permission to the volunteers to return to the hall.

This report was passed to Lieutenant General Bryan Mahon, the Commander-in-Chief of the British forces in Ireland, and he decided to order a search of the Larkfield complex on the basis that the premises was being used to manufacture and store explosives. On 14 February the DMP mustered two inspectors, four sergeants, and 50 police officers with three transport wagons to raid the premises, but for some unknown reason it was cancelled without explanation.

Undeterred, the DMP continued their surveillance on Larkfield, and on the evening of 15 February they observed 130 men, with seven of them carrying rifles, coming from the direction of Dolphin's Barn and entering the Hall. As the men arrived, they posted sentries in the trees at the entrance gates to the Larkfield Mill and set up a patrol of six men with bicycles to guard the perimeter of the premises. Owen Brien was now adamant that the Larkfield Mill should be closed down. He said that while the volunteers 'had not been aggressive in Dublin for some time', it should be closed down because they were 'beginning to assume a defiant attitude'.[22] An order was served by the military authorities on Count and Countess Plunkett; it appears that they ignored it and the volunteers continued to use the mill.

Within a week, on 24 February, two DMP men, Sergeant Johnson and Constable Curran, were on duty at Larkfield and they observed about 130 volunteers entering the hall about 10 a.m. They made a report to Supt Cornelius Kiernan of the Rathmines Divisional District, who responded by organizing a raiding party. By the time it arrived, the men had left the hall in twos and threes by going out through the fields at the rear of the hall, which backed on to the Dublin mountains. Kiernan believed that it was now imperative that the hall should be rendered unusable and he mustered another raiding party. This raiding party comprised 50 constables, a Chief Superintendent, an Inspector, and two lorries full of soldiers. This search party discovered bullets, spent bullet cartridges, broken bullets, paper targets, material for morse code lessons and spent bullets embedded in the walls, indicating that the volunteers regularly used the hall as a rifle range. The police took the material to Dublin Castle, and Supt Kiernan reported that:

> It is the opinion of the police and the soldiers who drove us in the lorries to Larkfield that some of the bullet marks are of very recent date and this opinion is very much strengthened by the fact that we found beneath the marks on the wall, lying on the floor ... some used up cartridges.[23]

On 1 March 1918, the military placed a permanent guard on the Larkfield Mill complex. However, there was a shortage of troops and Major W.P. Ball, the General Officer Commanding the Dublin District, suggested that in the interests of public safety the military should take possession of Larkfield and destroy the building. They then began the task of rendering the mill and bakery buildings unusable by bricking up the windows, demolishing the outside stairway, and removing some of the wood floorboards.

On 17 March 1917, Thomas Dillon, in the company of the officer in charge of the military guard at Larkfield, inspected the chemical plant and building. Accompanied by Lieutenant Bird of the 7th Royal Gloucesters he inspected the four-story building and examined the chemicals therein. Dillon wanted to sell the chemicals and had sought a permit to enable him bring prospective buyers to the plant. Lieutenant Bird saw no reason why he should not be allowed to do this, but the DMP disagreed. While he was satisfied that there were no arms and ammunition at the mill, Supt Kiernan thought that the vacuum still, the machinery, and the acid should be examined by an expert and that the Excise Authorities should be asked if they had any objection to the disposal of the chemicals. The issue now came to a halt, as Dillon and O'Connor were refused permission to enter the mill or to dispose of the chemicals.

Subsequently the military guard was removed from Larkfield and a plan was set in motion to divide the pastureland into allotments. This was carried out under the Tillage Orders Order 1918 to enhance food production in the city. The pastureland of Larkfield was now passed to the Irish Local Government Board, to be divided into 75 allotments.[24] Mr Berkley, secretary of the City Land Cultivation Committee, was given the responsibility for dividing the land and he asked for a police presence because he feared a boycott might take place. When Berkley arrived at Larkfield to take over the land James O'Neill refused to give him the keys of the entrance gate, but Berkley simply ordered his men to cross the railings. The reason O'Neill gave for refusing to open the gate was because there were 11 cows grazing on the land and these were the property of Countess Plunkett.

On 28 March 1918, Supt Kiernan went to Larkfield to observe the division of the land where he met the officer in charge, Lieutenant E. Bigley of the Gloucester Hussars. He was informed that earlier in the day, an unidentified man arrived at Larkfield to take possession of the land but he did not have a military permit and he was refused access to the mill. The DMP complied with the request for support and the division of the pastureland of the Larkfield Townland into 75 plots was completed that evening. By 6 May 1918, the military had left Larkfield and responsibility for surveillance of the boarded-up mill complex transferred to the DMP. By this time, the property was mortgaged to a Miss Moran to secure repayments of a loan of £1,500. Countess Plunkett had paid the initial deposit on Larkfield in 1913 but she failed to keep up the mortgage repayments.

In late March 1919, the Larkfield Mill, including the old bakery building, was sold by the mortgage holder. The advertisement for the auction described it as 'an extensive stone-built commercial building with about 1,000 feet floor space with its own continuous water supply' (presumably the Poddle).[25] Larkfield House and the six cottages were also sold, along with 13½ acres of land.

Countess Plunkett put the contents of the Larkfield Mill complex up for auction. This sale included 'plant and machinery, timber, baulk of pitch pine, building materials, chemical plant, gas holder, scrap iron, plus a Brougham harness, and a Kerry cow'.[26] The Plunkett family ceased to have any connection with the Larkfield townland.

# Epilogue

In 1919, there were two businesses in the Larkfield Complex: the Larkfield Saw Mill and Joinery Works and a woollen mill. Mr Cleary owned the latter and he was living in Larkfield House. The final raid on Larkfield by the military took place in March 1920 but nothing incriminating was discovered. In 1922, A.E. Derrington established a paint and varnish manufactory in the Larkfield Mill. By this time the townland, now on the cusp of change, was to become part of a new expansion of urban Dublin.

### Table 4. Occupiers at Larkfield, 1912–44

| Years | Occupiers | Official address | Business |
|---|---|---|---|
| 1910 | Herron Connolly Ltd | Larkfield Mill | miller merchant / roller mills |
| 1911 | | Larkfield Mill, 6 Dark Lane | |
| 1912–14 | Quinn | Larkfield Mill | baker and poplin weaver |
| 1914 | Quinn | | baker and poplin weaver |
| 1916–21 | Plunkett | | |
| 1923–30 | B. & K. Cleary | Larkfield Mill | Woollen manufacturers |
| 1938–44 | A.E. Derrington Ltd | Larkfield Mill– 12/18 Sundrive Rd. | St Kevin's Paint works (paint varnish colour manufacturer) |
| 1969 | A.E. Derrington Ltd | " " | Paint manufacturer |
| 1985–2010 | | Larkfield Mill site | Sundrive Shopping Centre |

Source: Land Valuation Office Dublin, the Registry of Deeds Dublin, *Irish Times*, *Thom's directory* and 1911 Census.

In 1928 the new Electricity Supply Board built 14 transformer stations around Dublin and one was located in the Tonguefield townland on the boundary with Larkfield. Under the Local Government (Dublin) Act of 1930, the Rathmines and Rathgar Township became part of the City of Dublin and its administration was taken over by Dublin City Corporation. In 1935, as part of the development of the city's western arterial road system, Dark Lane (which was a *cul-de-sac*) was opened up and Sundrive Road was created as a direct link to the Crumlin Road near Dolphin's Barn bridge.

During the 1940s under the Houses of the Working Classes Act, 1899–1931, the Larkfield townland was subsumed into the urbanization of rural South Dublin, when Dublin Corporation acquired a significant area of the Kimmage Road that included some of the land of the Larkfield townland.[1]

The current Larkfield housing estate is not located in the Larkfield townland. It is in fact located in the Kimmage townland. In 1932, the Building Operatives Public Utility Society built eight houses in Kimmage and called it Larkfield Gardens; apparently, at that time Larkfield was considered a more upmarket address than Kimmage. In 1933 the Dublin Building Operatives Society applied to build 76 houses and in 1934, the Post Office Public Utility Society built 32 houses. At some point, the Soldiers and Sailors and Landmark Trust (British Legion) also built a number of houses in the area. While Larkfield House, the Mill and some of the cottages survived until the late 1960s, the story of its role in 1916 has been lost. A new urban park dedicated to Eamon Ceannt, leader of the 4th Battalion, Irish Volunteers, was developed on Sundrive Road, but there is nothing to indicate that the men of the Kimmage Garrison ever existed. Today, there is a shopping centre on the site of Larkfield House and Mill with the river Poddle channelled underneath. The houses built on the pastureland of the Larkfield townland include part of Sundrive Road, Tonguefield Road, Blarney Road, and Poddle Park.

# Appendices

## Location and occupiers of buildings in Henry Place and Moore Place, 1916

| Number | Occupier | Businesses and homes |
| --- | --- | --- |
| 1 | Dundon Brothers | tenement house and workrooms |
| 2 | tenement | tenement |
| 3 | Elizabeth Brady | front room ground floor |
| 4/5 | Michael O'Brien and Co | mineral water company |
| 6 | "      " | mineral water company |
| 7 | "      " | mineral water company |
| 8 | "      " | mineral water company |
| 9 | lodgers | tenement |
| 10 | lodgers | tenement |
| 10a | Michael O'Brien | stores |
| 11,12,13 | Michael O'Brien | stable and loft (mineral water company) |
| 14 | vacant | |
| 16 | vacant | |
| 1/5 | Moore Place | tenements |

APPENDIX 2

## The section of Moore Street taken over by retreating rebel army in 1916

| House no. | Occupiers | Business |
|---|---|---|
| 10 | T.F. Cogan | provision dealer (house yard & shop) |
| 11 | James Plunkett | china and glass dealer (house yard & shop) |
| 12 | T.F. Cogan | confectionary (upper house & yard tenement) |
| 13 | Mrs R. A. Hogan | lodgers (upper house & yard) |
| 14 | Mrs Norton | china glass warehouse |
| 15 | Miss M. O'Gorman. | clothier dealer (house yard & shop ) |
| 16 | Patrick Plunkett | poulterer (upper house & yard tenement) |
| 17 | R.J. Gore | chemist and druggist |
| 18–19 | Ruins | |
| 20–21 | M. & P. Hanlon | fishmongers and ice merchants |
| 22, 23 | Prices Stores | glass, earthenware, fancy baskets etc |
| 24, 25 | Patrick Kelly | fish merchant |
| 24, 25 | Miss Matassa | ice cream Sackville Lane intersects |
| 26 | McCormack & Fogarty | grocers tea wine and spirit merchant |
| 27 | tenements | |
| 27a | M. Rhumann | pork butcher |
| 28 | Byrne Thomas | delph and china merchant |
| 29 | Thomas Melling | fruiterer |
| 30 | P. O'Connor | poulterer |
| 31/32 | Christopher Flanagan | poulterer Parnell Street intersects |

Source: Land Valuation Office Dublin, the Registry of deeds Dublin and *Thom's directory* 1901–22

APPENDIX 3

## The membership of the Kimmage Garrison

| Forename | Surname | Location |
|---|---|---|
| Arthur | Agnew | Manchester |
| David | Begley | Manchester |
| John | Bolger | Liverpool |
| James | Bolger | Liverpool |
| Peadear | Bracken | Tullamore |
| (2) | Breaslin | Glasgow |
| (1) | Breaslin | Glasgow |
| Seamus | Brennan | Tullamore |
| Patrick | Caldwell | Liverpool |
| Charles | Caragan | Liverpool |
| S. | Carmichael | Glasgow |
| John | Carroll | Liverpool |
| Patrick J. | Clinch | Liverpool |
| Joseph (Jerry Malone) | Coghlan | Manchester |
| Michael | Collins | London |
| Thomas | Craven | Liverpool |
| Denis | Daly | London |
| Liam | Daly | London |
| William | Dickenson | Liverpool |
| Joseph | Duffy | Liverpool |
| Joseph | Egan | Liverpool |
| Francis | Flanagan | Dublin |
| Michael | Flanagan | Dublin |
| Bernard | Friel | Glasgow |
| Andrew | Furlong | London |
| Matthew | Furlong | Manchester |
| Joseph | Gahan | Dublin |
| Martin | Gleeson | Liverpool |
| Joseph | Gleeson | Liverpool |
| Alfred Joseph | Good | London |
| John | Harling | London |
| Seán | Hegarty | Glasgow |
| John | Horan | Not stated |
| Con. | Keating | London |
| Frank | Kelly | Manchester |
| Gilbert | Kennan | London |
| Niall Jr | Kerr | Liverpool |
| John | Kerr | Liverpool |
| Thomas | Kerr | Liverpool |
| John | King | Liverpool |
| Patrick | King | Liverpool |
| George | King | Liverpool |
| Seamus | Landy | Liverpool |
| Gilbert | Lynch | Manchester |
| Patrick J. (White) | Maguire | Glasgow |
| Garrett | McAuliffe | Manchester |

| Forename | Surname | Location |
|----------|---------|----------|
| Patrick | McDermott | Liverpool |
| John | McGallogly | Glasgow |
| Seamus | McGallogly | Glasgow |
| Milo | McGarry | Glasgow |
| Michael | McGarvey | Liverpool |
| Michael | McGrath | London |
| Liam | McGinley | Glasgow & New York |
| Patrick | McMahon | Liverpool |
| Patrick | McManus | Liverpool |
| Braun | McMullen | Glasgow |
| William | McNeive | Liverpool |
| Patrick | Morrin | Glasgow |
| Michael | Mulvihill | Manchester |
| Michael | Murphy | Glasgow |
| Victor | Murphy | Liverpool |
| Michael | Murphy | Manchester |
| Ernest | Nunan | London |
| Seán | Nunan | London |
| John (Blimey) | O'Connor | London |
| Seamus | O'Donnagáin | Manchester |
| Seamus | O'Donnaghadha | Manchester |
| William | O'Donoghue | Liverpool |
| Patrick | O'Donoghue | Manchester |
| James | O'Dowd | Liverpool |
| Diarmuid | O'Leary | London |
| David | O'Leary | London |
| Tomás | O'Murchadha | Liverpool |
| Joseph | O'Reilly | London |
| Michael | O'Shea | Liverpool |
| Liam | Parr | Manchester |
| George Officer I/C | Plunkett | Dublin |
| Seamus | Robinson | Glasgow |
| Liam | Roche | Liverpool |
| Laurence | Ryan | Manchester |
| Frank | Scullion | Glasgow |
| Patrick | Scullion | Glasgow |
| Dona | Sheehan | London |
| Patrick | Shortis | London |
| Pádraig | Supple | Liverpool |
| Hugh | Thornton | Liverpool |
| Patrick | Thornton | London |
| Cormac | Turner | Glasgow |
| Cormac | Turner | Glasgow |
| Joseph | Vise | Liverpool |
| Martin | Walsh | Liverpool |
| Gilbert | Ward | Liverpool |
| Christopher | Whelehan | Liverpool |

*Sources*: BMH, Witness statements by Seamus Robinson, Joe Good, John McGallogly, Arthur Agnew, UCDA archive, Joe Robinson's personal account in Eithne Coyle papers.

# Notes

## ABBREVIATIONS

| | |
|---|---|
| BMH | Bureau of Military History |
| CD | Contemporaneous Documents |
| CO | Colonial Office, The National Archives, London |
| DMP | Dublin Metropolitan Police |
| IMA | Irish Military Archives |
| NAL | National Archives London |
| RIC | Royal Irish Constabulary |
| UCDA | University College Dublin Archives |
| WO | War Office |

### 1. LARKFIELD HOUSE AND MILL, 1837–1913

1  *Irish Times*, 29 Mar. 1899.
2  Ibid.
3  Ibid., 9 June 1890.
4  Geraldine Plunkett Dillon, *All in the blood: a memoir of the Plunkett family, the 1916 Rising and the war of Independence*, ed. Honor O'Brolchain (Dublin, 2006), pp 151–2.
5  Ibid., 151.
6  IMA, BMH W[itness] S[tatement ] 488 (Jack Plunkett), p. 15.
7  Dillon, *All in the blood*, p. 151.

### 2. THE IRISH VOLUNTEERS AND THE CREATION OF THE KIMMAGE GARRISON

1  *Irish Volunteer*, 18 April 1914, p. 9.
2  Dillon, *All in the blood*, p. 165.
3  Ernie O'Malley, *On another man's wound* (Dublin, 1936), p. 46.
4  Dillon, *All in the blood*, p. 165.

5  Ibid., p. 156.
6  IMA, BMH WS 152 (Arthur Agnew), p. 2.
7  Ibid., p. 1.
8  IMA, BMH WS 367 (Joseph Gleeson), p. 1.
9  Joe Good, *Enchanted by dreams: the journal of a revolutionary* (Kerry, 1996), p. 8.
10  John (Blimey) O'Connor, personal memoir, p. 2.
11  Ibid.
12  Ibid.
13  Margaret Skinnider, *Doing my bit for Ireland* (New York, 1917), p. 9.
14  IMA, BMH WS 156 (Seamus Robinson), p. 9.
15  Ibid.
16  IMA, BMH WS 244 (John McGallogly), p. 1.
17  Colonial Office confidential intelligence report, National Archives London, CO/903/19.
18  IMA, BMH WS 156 (Seamus Robinson), p. 9.
19  IMA, BMH WS 356 (Milo McGarry), p. 6.
20  Dillon, *All in the blood*, pp 197–8.

21  Ibid.
22  IMA, BMH WS 156 (Seamus Robinson), p. 13.
23  IMA, BMH WS 244 (John McGallogly), p. 4.
24  Ibid.
25  Ibid., p. 6.
26  IMA, BMH WS 388 (Joe Good), p. 3.
27  Tim Pat Coogan, *Michael Collins* (London, 1990), p. 29.
28  Good, *Enchanted by dreams*, p. 9.
29  IMA, BMH WS 110 (Denis Daly), p. 2.
30  Dillon, *All in the blood*, p. 195.
31  Ibid.

### 3. LIFE AT THE KIMMAGE VOLUNTEER CAMP

1  Dillon, *All in the blood*, p. 190.
2  IMA, BMH WS 388 (Joe Good), p. 3.
3  IMA, BMH WS 244 (John McGallogly), p. 7.
4  Dillon, *All in the Blood*, p. 190.

5 Ibid., p. 190.
6 IMA, BMH WS 244 (John McGallogly), p. 6.
7 O'Connor, personal memoir, p. 3.
8 Ibid.
9 IMA, BMH WS 388 (Joe Good), p. 4.
10 Ibid.
11 IMA, BMH WS 244 (John McGallogly), p. 6.
12 IMA, BMH WS 388 (Joe Good), p. 4.
13 Ibid.
14 IMA, BMH WS 361 (Peadar Bracken ), p. 2.
15 Ibid.
16 Ibid.
17 *Irish Times*, 25 Mar. 1916.
18 Ibid.
19 Ibid.
20 Ibid.
21 Ibid.
22 IMA, BMH WS 152 (Arthur P. Agnew), p. 3.
23 IMA, BMH WS 110 (Denis Daly), p. 1.
24 *Irish Times*, 29 Apr. 1916.
25 IMA, BMH WS 152 (Arthur P. Agnew), p. 3.
26 O'Connor, personal memoir, p. 4.
27 IMA, BMH WS 152 (Arthur P. Agnew), p. 3.
28 Dillon, *All in the blood*, p. 221
29 IMA, BMH WS 367 (Joseph Gleeson), p. 8.

4. THE CHAOS OF REBELLION

1 IMA, BMH WS 152 (Seamus Robinson), p. 14.
2 IMA, BMH WS 367 (Joseph Gleeson), p. 8.
3 IMA, BMH WS 152 (Seamus Robinson), p. 14.
4 IMA, BMH WS 152 (Arthur Agnew), p. 3.
5 IMA, BMH WS 152 (Arthur P. Agnew), p. 3.

6 IMA, BMH WS 244 (John McGallogly), p. 7.
7 O'Connor, personal memoir, p. 4.
8 Seamus Robinson, personal account (undated) (UCDA, Coyle papers, p 61/13 (14)).
9 IMA, BMH WS 388 (Joe Good), p. 6.
10 Ann Matthews, 'Vanguard of the Revolution' in Ruan O'Donnell (ed.), *The impact of the 1916 Rising: among the nations* (Dublin, 2008), p. 31.
11 IMA, BMH WS 152 (Arthur P. Agnew), p. 4.
12 IMA, BMH WS 110 (Denis Daly), p. 4.
13 IMA, BMH WS 388 (Joe Good), p. 6.
14 Ibid., pp 6–7.
15 IMA, BMH WS 358 (Geraldine Plunkett Dillon), p. 16
16 Ibid., p. 17.
17 Ibid., p. 18.
18 IMA, BMH WS 699 (Josephine Clarke), p. 8.
19 Ann Devlin Branch Glasgow, 1916–22 (UCDA, Coyle papers. p 61/4 (67)), p. 1.
20 IMA, BMH WS 497 (Eamon Bulfin), p. 7.
21 Ibid.
22 IMA, BMH WS 497 (R.H. Walpole & Theobald Fitzgerald), p. 2.
23 Ibid.
24 Ibid.
25 G.A. Hayes McCoy, *A history of Irish flags from earliest times* (Dublin, 1979), p. 218.
26 IMA, BMH WS 497 (R.H. Walpole & Theobald Fitzgerald), p. 7.
27 *Dublin Saturday Post*, 29 Apr. and 6, 13 May 1916.
28 IMA MBH WS (Arthur P. Agnew), p. 4.

29 Ibid., p. 4.
30 IMA, BMH WS 110 (Denis Daly), p. 4.
31 IMA, BMH WS 93 W.J. (May McLoughlin), p. 2.
32 IMA, BMH WS 568 (Eilish Ní Chonaill (*nee* Ní Riain)), p. 9.
33 Ibid.
34 Tom Stanley, *Joe Stanley: printer to the rising* (Co. Kerry, 2005), p. 43.
35 IMA, BMH WS 398 (Brigid Martin), p. 9.
36 IMA, BMH WS 361 (Peadar Bracken), p. 8.
37 W.J. Brennan-Whitmore, *Dublin burning: the Easter Rising from behind the barricades* (Dublin, 1996), p. 4.
38 Ibid.
39 James Stephens, *Insurrection in Dublin* (Dublin 1916), pp 26–7.
40 Ibid., p. 60.
41 IMA, BMH WS 398 (Brigid Martin), p. 9.

5. RETREAT AND SURRENDER

1 Colonial Office Confidential Intelligence report (NA London, com papers CO/903/19).
2 *Dublin Saturday Post*, 29 Apr. and 6, 13 May 1916.
3 Ibid.
4 IMA, BMH WS 244 (John McGallogly), p. 9.
5 IMA, BMH WS 497 (Eamon Bulfin), p. 497.
6 IMA, BMH Ws 488 (Jack Plunkett), p. 30.
7 IMA, BMH WS 388 (Joe Good), p. 10.
8 IMA, BMH WS 152 (Arthur Agnew), p. 6.
9 IMA, BMH WS 388 (Joe Good), p. 11.
10 Ibid., p. 11.

11  Ibid.
12  Ibid., p. 12.
13  Ibid.
14  Good, *Enchanted by dreams*, pp 56–7.
15  William Mullen, death certificate. General Register Office Dublin.
16  Good, *Enchanted by dreams*, p. 58.
17  IMA, BMH WS 899 (Seamus ua Coamhanaigh), p. 57.
18  Ibid.
19  Ibid.
20  Ibid., p. 58.
21  *Dublin Saturday Post*, 29 Apr. and 6, 13 May 1916.
22  IMA, BMH WS 497 (Eamonn Bulfin), p. 1.
23  John (Blimey) O'Connor, personal statement, p. 8.
24  Ibid.
25  IMA, BMG WS (Eamonn Bulfin), p. 12.
26  IMA, BMH WS 361 (Peadar Bracken), p. 12.
27  IMA, BMH WS 899 (Seamus ua Coamhanaigh), p. 60.
28  Elizabeth O'Farrell, 'Events of Easter week' in *Catholic Bulletin* (Apr. 1917), 267.
29  Ibid.
30  Ibid.
31  IMA, BMH Brother Allen (CD. 75/1/4).
32  Julia Grennan, 'Account of Easter week, undated' in *Catholic Bulletin* 7:6 (April 1917), 396.

33  *Dublin Saturday Post*, 29 Apr. and 6, 13 May 1916.
34  Ibid.
35  IMA, BMH WS 162 (John Shouldice), p. 10.
36  'Applications for souvenirs', War Office files (National Archives London, WO 35/69).
37  Ibid.
38  IMA, BMH WS 244 (John McGallogly), p. 12.
39  Eamonn Bulfin, mobilization order (IMA MBH CD 99/1).
40  IMA, BMH WS 244 (John McGallogly), p. 13.
41  Ibid.
42  Dublin Castle Special Branch files, 13 September 1916 (CO/213/359), pp 70–1.
43  Ibid.
44  Ibid, 5 June 1916, p. 41.

6. THE LARKFIELD
CHEMICAL COMPANY AND
THE BRITISH AUTHORITIES

1  Dublin Castle Special Branch files, 25 July 1916 (CO/213/360), p. 128.
2  Ibid.
3  Ibid., p. 147.
4  Dillon, *All in the blood*, p. 234.
5  Dublin Castle Special Branch files, 22 August 1916 (CO/213/360), p. 126.
6  Ibid., 14 Sept. 1916, p. 116.

7  Ibid.
8  Ibid.
9  Ibid.
10  Ibid., p. 141.
11  Ibid.
12  Ibid.
13  Grace Gifford Plunkett, witness statement, (MA, BMH, WS 257), p. 1.
14  Dillon, *All in the blood*, p. 247.
15  Dublin Castle Special Branch files (CO/213/359), p. 77.
16  Ibid., pp 73–4.
17  Dublin Castle Special Branch files, 29 December 1916 (CO/213/359), p. 57.
18  Ibid., 15 Jan. 1917, p. 48.
19  Ibid.
20  Michael Laffan, *The Resurrection of Ireland: the Sinn Féin Part, 1916–1923* (Cambridge, 1999), p. 93.
21  Dublin Castle Special Branch files, 6 February 1918 (CO/904/213/360), p. 114.
22  Ibid., 15 Feb. 1918, p. 106.
23  Ibid., 25 Feb. 1918, p. 79.
24  Ibid., 8 Mar. 1918.
25  Ibid., 8 Mar. 1919, p. 12.
26  *Irish Times*, 23 Apr. 1919.

EPILOGUE

1  Dublin Corporation (Crumlin South (No. 2) (Captains Lane)), Extension Compulsory Purchase Order, 1945.